Crisis, Globalization and Governance

Crisis, Globalization and Governance: How to Draw Lessons?

Edited by

Nehme Azoury and Frank Bournois

CAMBRIDGE SCHOLARS

PUBLISHING

Crisis, Globalization and Governance: How to Draw Lessons?,
Edited by Nehme Azoury and Frank Bournois

This book first published 2014

Cambridge Scholars Publishing

12 Back Chapman Street, Newcastle upon Tyne, NE6 2XX, UK

British Library Cataloguing in Publication Data
A catalogue record for this book is available from the British Library

ISBN (10): 1-4438-5660-6, ISBN (13): 978-1-4438-5660-7

TABLE OF CONTENTS

LIST OF TABLES AND FIGURES

FOREWORD

The articles that comprise this volume are a selection from the valuable contributions of scholars to the 'Crisis, Globalization and Governance: How to Draw Lessons?' International Conference hosted, on the 2nd to the 3rd of April 2012, by the Holy Spirit University of Kaslik and the Arab Society of Faculties of Business, Economics and Political Sciences.

The seven contributions focus on specific forms of governance in the private and public sectors which aim to redirect the globalization process in a healthier and more efficient way. Globalization has turned a fully diversified world into a huge melting pot where innovations and technological breakthroughs play a fundamental role in restructuring the governance of organizations. Organizations have to adapt to the best practices that fit into their culture, and to prevent changes happening on the global level in order to avoid the risk of losing their competitive advantages.

The contributions focus on issues of globalization from a cross-cultural perspective. The articles relate to the following fields: Globalization, Leadership and Governance, Corporate Social Responsibility, University Governance, Management of Information Systems, and Social Entrepreneurship. Dealing with a multidisciplinary conference, this book will be of interest to a wide readership: academics, administrators and business executives, as well as management students. It highlights the diversity of development experiences and suggests that there cannot be a single path to progress in spite of globalization.

The Impact of Globalization on Islamic Countries: A Brief Assessment

Khan Habibullah

Abstract

After briefly discussing the various issues pertaining to globalization and the global economy, this paper presents the comparative economic performance of Islamic countries by using appropriate statistics, and discusses the challenges, mainly the economic ones. It is stressed that Islamic countries, or at least a subset of them, have great potential and would benefit from globalization, if they can successfully upgrade their young labour force through various education and training programmes. Although steps are being taken in the right direction in some Islamic countries (particularly GCC countries), more comprehensive measures are required for human capital formation to meet the needs of today's knowledge-based economy.

Keywords: Globalization, Knowledge-based economy, Indicators of globalization, Islamic countries, GCC countries, Education, Life-long learning.

Introduction

Globalization can be defined as the process through which the free flow of ideas, people, goods, services and capital leads to the integration of economies and societies. The world has experienced successive waves of globalization going back as far as Marco Polo in the thirteenth century. The term 'globalization' here is viewed strictly in terms of relevant economic indicators.[1] The focus is on the impact of the most recent (after the 'Information and Communications Technology' or ICT revolution) wave of globalization. The ICT revolution in the 1970s greatly facilitated the exchange and processing of information by expanding the range and quality of services that can be traded, moving us towards a 'global village'.

While traditional economic theory (based on the assumptions of free trade) suggests that a fully integrated world economy provides the greatest scope for maximizing human welfare, the contemporary literature highlights the benefits of knowledge sharing and dissemination through information technology. The importance of a knowledge-based economy (KBE) was emphasized by the World Bank (1998):

> *'For countries in the vanguard of the world economy, the balance between knowledge and resources has shifted so far toward the former that knowledge has become perhaps the most important factor determining the standard of living – more than land, than tools, than labor. Today's most technologically advanced economies are truly knowledge-based. And as they generate new wealth from their innovations, they are creating millions of knowledge-related jobs in an array of disciplines that have emerged overnight.'* (*The World Development Report: Knowledge for Development* 1998/99, p. 16)

Knowledge is power; with the help of cross-border sharing of knowledge, the global economy is becoming more integrated and countries cannot be reluctant in this regard. Multinational corporations (MNCs) are becoming too dominant in the global landscape, and approximately one-third of global trade is now between MNCs and their affiliates. More than 50% of GDP in major OECD countries is based on the production and distribution of knowledge. Information technologies are advancing at a

---

[1] Globalization may have a mixed impact on the welfare of the members of society. According to Johnson (2002), economic liberalization, or globalization in a broader context, is expected to bring benefits to the developing countries, in terms of both static and dynamic gains. For instance, trade reform through diffusion of knowledge and technology in the past benefited the world's poor enormously (e.g. great increase in life expectancy, reduction of child mortality, doubling of grain yield, increase in per capita food supply, etc.). However, trade liberalization may not be welfare-improving in all cases. Bannister and Thugge (2001) emphasized the possibility of gainers and losers in trade reforms. They noted that trade liberalization causes restructuring and dislocation, and people with few assets may suffer adverse effects from trade reforms due to adjustment costs.

tremendous rate and a country can create dynamic comparative advantage by improving its distinctive knowledge:

> *'While nature shows a tendency to diminishing return, man shows a tendency to increasing return. Knowledge is our most powerful engine of production; it enables us to subdue nature and satisfy our wants.'* (Alfred Marshall, quoted in *The World Development Report: Knowledge for Development* 1998/99, pp. 20–21)

The World Bank has advised developing countries to acquire and adapt global knowledge and create knowledge locally, to invest in human capital in order to increase the ability to absorb and use knowledge, and to invest in technologies that facilitate both the acquisition and the absorption of knowledge.

The structure for this paper is as follows: after introductory remarks on globalization and the knowledge-based economy in section 1, we discuss Muslims' perception of globalization in section 2; in section 3 we provide a snapshot of the global economy and discuss Islamic countries' share of the global economy; the global economic outlook is discussed in section 4, and the prospect and impact of globalization are discussed in section 5; section 6 concludes the paper.

1. Muslims' Perception of Globalization

Economic liberalization or globalization opens the borders of societies to the culture of foreign markets as well as for the individualism and the consumerism that go with it. Global culture tends to homogenize societies along the lines of a Western model that does not always fit well with local culture. Islamic countries are no exception.

There is a lack of independent scientific and technological research in these countries, and they are reliant on foreign aid/capital. Most Muslim countries are dependent on the West for technological infrastructure (machinery, equipment, medicine, etc.) and high-quality consumer and luxury goods. The liberalization of technological diffusion and innovation guarantees that Muslim countries will be permanently dependent on the West, which is seen negatively by the 'Dependency school of thought'.

There has been a negative perception of globalization in the Muslim world. Globalization/westernization may inculcate young people locally with Western values and ideas (e.g. unacceptable moral standards in movies, music, dance). Islam is seen as being marginalized from global processes as global politics is dominated by the United States. Islamic countries are predominantly state-controlled and Western-style democracy is not seen positively in the Muslim world. The core of globalization, which preaches universalism, inclusiveness and pragmatism, is not consistent with Islamic faith based on Muslim brotherhood and Shariah.

For instance, Islamic teachings prohibit the interest on loans (*riba al-qurud*) and on savings accounts, ban speculation due to the uncertainty and lack of transparency involved (*gharar*), emphasize adherence to risk-sharing and profit-sharing as well as promotion of socially responsible and ethical investments that are conducive to the welfare of society. These are in contrast to Western principles of economic freedom based on materialism.

Is it possible to change the negative perception of globalization in the Muslim world? The answer is perhaps 'yes'. Islam is the first religion to make acquisition of knowledge obligatory for both Muslim men and Muslim women, even in far-off places like China. Of course, there are challenges, and the lack of ICT infrastructure, manpower and academic resources in the Islamic world makes it difficult to acquire knowledge. Adapting education to the growing needs of the job market is of paramount importance. 'Freedom' is necessary to promote creativity within education, and this is in line with Islamic Civilization (Muslim scholars and religious leaders used to hold intellectual discourse/sessions at mosques). The ICT revolution (or global flow of information) can forge closer links with heterogeneous Muslim communities, and more cooperation and understanding between them can be expected as an outcome.

The Quran emphasizes justice, equality, compassion and peace, apart from knowledge and wisdom, and Islamic countries/scholars may seize this opportunity to promote these values worldwide in order to erase current misgivings and help establish a true 'global village'. Islam does not encourage 'extremes', and Muslims are advised to follow the 'middle path' (moderation).

Modern education and religious practices can be combined to create prosperous Muslim societies, while research in science and technology can be encouraged as far as they contribute to peace and prosperity. Islam believes in the peaceful coexistence of all (including people of other religions) rather than the 'Islamization' of the whole world. It is important that we understand the distinction between 'Fundamentalism' (based on 'five' fundamental 'pillars' of Islam) and 'fanaticism' (radicalization of Islamic beliefs to 'extremes' that could lead to hatred of other religions).

2. Islamic Countries in the Global Economy

The global economy is dominated by high-income countries. In terms of real GDP (PPP-based), they account for 57% of world output (the US alone captures 21%; Japan 6%), whereas China contributes 12 % to global GDP and India's share is about 5%. In terms of growth rates, China and India have accounted for more than one third of global GDP growth in recent years. The Chinese economy was worth US$7.9 trillion in 2008 PPP terms. The Indian economy was equivalent to US$3.4 trillion. In per capita real terms, the average income in China is US$ 6,020 ($2,940 in 2010 market prices) and that of India is only US$ 2,960 ($1,070 in market prices). Both are classified as 'Lower-middle income' countries (World Bank, *The World Development Report 2010*, pp. 378–79).

Muslim countries are spread across regions: the Middle East and North Africa, Sub-Saharan Africa, South Asia, East Asia, and Europe and Central Asia. The bulk of Islamic countries fall into the category of low-income countries (LIC) with income of $975 or less, and lower-middle income countries (LMC) with income ranging between $976 and $3,855. Only a few Islamic countries are classified as 'upper-middle income' (UMC) with an income range of $3,856 to $11,905, or 'high-income' (above $11,906) (World Bank, 2010). Table 1 shows the World Bank classification of Islamic countries.

Table 1.1 World Bank Classifications of Islamic Countries

Categories	Countries
Low-income (LIC) US$975 or less	Afghanistan, Bangladesh, Benin, Burkina Faso, Chad, Comoros, Gambia, Guinea-Bissau, Mali, Mauritania, Mozambique, Niger, Senegal, Sierra Leone, Somalia, Togo, Yemen Republic.
Lower-middle income (LMC) US$ 976 to 3,855	Albania, Cameroon, Cote d'Ivoire, Djibouti, Egypt, Iran, Iraq, Jordan, Morocco, Nigeria, Sudan, Syria, Arab Rep. Tunisia, West Bank and Gaza, Indonesia, Maldives, Pakistan, Turkey.
Upper-middle income (UMC) US$ 3,856 to $11,905	Algeria, Azerbaijan, Gabon, Kyrgiz Republic, Lebanon, Libya, Malaysia, Tajikistan.
High-income countries Above US$11,905	Bahrain, Brunei Darussalam, Kuwait, Oman, Qatar, Saudi Arabia, United Arab Emirates.

Source: World Bank, *The World Development Report 2010.*

The Islamic share of the global economic pie is quite low. The current share of the Middle East and North Africa (MENA) to global real income

(PPP$) is 3.4% (with an average per capita income of $7,308), and that of Sub-Saharan Africa is only 2.3% (with an average per capita income of $1,991). The whole of South Asia (including India, which has a large Muslim population) contributes only 6% to world GDP (with an average per capita real income of $2,734). Hassan et al. (2010) show that OIC (57 countries with roughly 20% of world population) contributed only 4.7% to total world real GDP during 1980–2007; the average income of OIC during this period was only $1,139 – far below the world average of $4,786. Noland and Pack (2004), citing Egypt as an example, also conclude that Islamic countries are far behind their rivals in the export of manufacturing products:

> *'Although Egypt has a population more than South Korea's and Taiwan's combined the Asian countries export more manufactures in two days than Egypt does in an entire year.'* (Noland, M. and Pack, H. 2004)

There has been some encouraging performance, too. The per capita wealth (produced capital and urban land, intangible capital, and natural capital) in some Islamic countries is quite respectable: Algeria ($18,491), Ivory Coast ($14,243), Egypt ($21,879), Indonesia ($13,869), Iran ($24,023), Malaysia ($46,687), Morocco ($22,965); these figures compare well with Asian giants such as China ($9,387) and India ($6,820). Intangible capital (raw labour, human capital, social capital, and quality of institutions) plays a critical role in Ivory Coast, Indonesia, Malaysia, Morocco and Egypt.[2]

We now turn our discussion to the success stories of some Islamic countries compared to developed nations. The Asian 'high-fliers' include Japan (US$38,210 and PPP $35,220), Hong Kong (US$31,420 and PPP $43,960) and Singapore (US$34,760 and PPP $47,940). Swiss income stands at a staggering US$65,330 (PPP $46,460), and that of the US is $47,580 (PPP $46,970). The per capita average income of 'High-income' economies (mostly OECD countries) is US$39,345 (PPP $37,141) (World Bank, 2010, pp. 378–79).

In comparison, the rich Gulf States (with the exception of Saudi Arabia and UAE) are classified by the World Bank as 'Other high income economies'. The latest per capita income figures are: Saudi Arabia US $15,500 (PPP $22,950), UAE $45,200 (in terms of PPP $), Bahrain PPP

---

[2] Sweden ($513,424) tops the list in per capita wealth followed by the US ($512,612); other wealthy countries include Germany ($496,447), Japan ($493,241), Austria ($493,080) and France ($468,024). World Bank, *The World Development Report 2010*, p. 368.

$23,100, Brunei Darussalam $26,740 (PPP $50,200), Kuwait $38,420 (PPP $52,610), Oman $12,270 (PPP $20,650), and Qatar PPP $26,300. Wikipedia ranks 57 OIC countries in terms of per capita real GDP, and UAE is at the top of the chart (followed by Qatar and Brunei; Somalia, Comoros and PLA are at the bottom, with PPP $600 per capita income).

In terms of HDI, Norway, Australia, Iceland, Canada and Ireland are the top five countries. Japan ranks 10, Hong Kong 24, and Singapore 23 (Human Development Report, 2009). China ranks 92 and India's position is 134 (within a total of 182 countries). GCC countries have achieved 'High human development' status (HDI index is above 0.80 for the first 83 selected countries) (United Nations Development Programme 2009, *Human Development Report: Overcoming Barriers – Human Mobility and Development*, New York). Table 2 shows the top 10 Islamic countries in real GDP and associated HDI.

Table 1.2 Top 10 Islamic Countries in Real GDP

Countries	GDP (PPP $)	HDI 2007 (Rank)
UAE	45,200	0.903 (35)
Qatar	28,300	0.910 (33)
Brunei	23,600	0.920 (30)
Bahrain	23,100	0.895 (39)
Kuwait	20,300	0.916 (31)
Oman	13,500	0.846 (56)
Turkey	13,138	0.806 (79)
Saudi Arabia	13,100	0.843 (59)
Malaysia	12,000	0.824 (66)
Libya	11,800	0.847 (55)

Source: United Nations Development Programme, *Human Development Report*, various issues, New York.

In terms of the Global Competitiveness Index (GCI) 2010–11, the top 5 countries are Switzerland, Sweden, Singapore, US and Germany. China and India ranked 27 and 51 respectively (out of 139 countries included in the survey). Nine OIC countries are within the top-50 list: Qatar ranks 17 (position improved by 5 places over 2009–10); Saudi Arabia ranks 21 (improved by 7 places over the previous years); UAE (25); Malaysia (26); Brunei Darussalam (28); Oman 34 (improved by 7 places over 2009): Kuwait 35 (improved by 4 places); Bahrain (37), and Indonesia ranks 44 (improved by 10 places over 2009–10) (World Economic Forum, *Global Competitiveness Report 2010–11*, Geneva). In terms of the Global Innovation Index (GII) 2009–10, the top 10 countries (out of 132 included in the study) are: Iceland, Sweden, Hong Kong, Switzerland, Denmark, Finland, Singapore, Netherlands, New Zealand and Norway. Asia's fastest-growing countries, China and India, occupy positions 43 and 56 respectively. There are a few Islamic countries in the list of top-50 innovators: UAE (24), Malaysia (28), Kuwait (33), Qatar (35), Bahrain (40), Brunei Darussalam (48), Saudi Arabia (54) and Oman (65) (INSEAD 2010, *Global Innovation Index Report 2009–10*, France). Table 3 shows the top 10 Islamic countries with their GCI and GII score (ranked in GCI):

Table 1.3.Top 10 Islamic Countries (ranked in GCI)

Countries	GCI 2010–11 Rank	GII 2009–10 Rank
Qatar	17	35
Saudi Arabia	21	54
UAE	25	24
Malaysia	26	28
Brunei Darussalam	28	48
Oman	34	65
Kuwait	35	33
Bahrain	37	40
Indonesia	44	72
Turkey	61	67

Sources: World Economic Forum, *Global Competitiveness Report 2010–11*, Geneva; and INSEAD, *Global Innovation Index Report 2009–10*, France.

We observe some surprising results in the Global Innovation Index 2009–10. The highest scorers are all small countries, while the US, the most populous country (with 4.54% of world population) among the first fifteen, ranks number 11. Iceland's performance in infrastructure and ICT pillars was the most outstanding, helping it to clinch the top position. It also did well in indicators related to human capacity, but its performance in investment and credit conditions was somewhat muted. Hong Kong's success can be attributed to the pillars of creative outputs and well-being, market sophistication and institutions. These indices also indicate that the US is losing its innovative edge. From its number-one position in 2009, the US slipped to 11th position in 2010.

Although America is slowly coming out of recession, it is facing stiff competition from other countries in maintaining its supremacy as a global powerhouse of education, science and technology. Paul Krugman recently cautioned that the American education standard is falling, and he asked for more funds to retain good teachers and educate bright children from less affluent families.

Another report adds that about half the engineering doctoral degrees in America are awarded to foreign nationals, and Asian countries like China and South Korea are producing large numbers of engineering graduates that are challenging the US strength in human capital (INSEAD 2010, p. 19).

There are some bright spots in the Islamic world. In the sub-pillar 'Knowledge Application' (growth rate of labour productivity, industry value added, production process sophistication, employment in knowledge-intensive services), the top performers include Qatar (1), Brunei-Darussalam (2) and Azerbaijan (4), along with traditional giants in the application of knowledge like Switzerland (7), USA (6) and Canada (9). Although Oman does not feature prominently in the overall innovation index, it does very well (11th position jointly with Ireland) in the sub-pillar 'Benefits to social welfare' (INSEAD 2010, p. 26).

The project 'Vision 2023: Turkey's Foreign Policy', which aims to build a knowledge-based society dedicated to the development of science and technology, and to hike its research and technology development expenditure to about 2% of GDP, gets special mention in the report (INSEAD 2010, p. 32).

According to the KOF Index of Globalization, Belgium, Austria, the Netherlands, Switzerland and Sweden are the most globalized countries in the world. Singapore ranks number 17 and is the only Asian country within the first 20 most globalized nations. China and India rank 63 and 111 respectively in terms of the overall index.

The OIC countries that are within the top-50 globalized countries include Malaysia (35), Jordan (36), Bahrain (41), Qatar (43) and Kuwait (47). Other Islamic countries that are moderately globalized include UAE (64), Egypt (68), Morocco (72), Saudi Arabia (74) and Indonesia (86) (*KOF Index of Globalization 2010*, ETH, Zurich).

The 5 freest economies in the world, according to the 2010 *Index of Economic Freedom*, are: Hong Kong, Singapore, Australia, New Zealand and Ireland. The USA holds 8th position and Japan ranks number 19 in the chart. The world's fastest-growing economies of China and India are still quite 'closed' and rank 140 and 124 respectively. The Islamic countries that feature prominently in the index are: Bahrain (13), Qatar (39), Kuwait (42), Oman (43), UAE (46), Jordan (52), Malaysia (59), Saudi Arabia (65) and Turkey (67) (*2010 Index of Economic Freedom*, The Heritage Foundation, and Washington, DC). Table 4 shows the top 10 Islamic countries ranked by Globalization.

Table 1.4 Top 10 Islamic Countries (Ranked by KOF Index of Globalization)

Countries	KOF Index of Globalization 2010	Index of Economic Freedom 2010
Malaysia	35	59
Jordan	36	52
Bahrain	41	13
Qatar	43	39
Kuwait	47	42
Lebanon	52	89
Turkey	56	67
UAE	64	46
Egypt	68	94
Saudi Arabia	74	65

Source: KOF Index of Globalization 2010, ETH, Zurich; *2010 Index of Economic Freedom*, the Heritage Foundation, and Washington, DC.

3. The Global Economic Outlook

The global income distribution is very uneven and has often been compared with a champagne glass. At the top, where the glass is widest, the richest 20% of the population hold three-quarters of world income. At the bottom, where the glass is narrowest, the poorest 40% hold 5% of world income, and the poorest 20% hold just 1.5%. The poorest 40% correspond to the 2 billion people living on less than $2 a day.

Following a sharp deterioration during late 2008 and early 2009, the global economy is now improving and stabilizing. Equity markets have rebounded, and trade and industrial production indices are showing upward trends in most countries. An increasing number of countries showed growth in the second half of 2009 and first half of 2010, but will the recovery lose steam? The outlook for the global economy remains uncertain, and conditions for sustained growth are rather fragile.

The International Monetary Fund (IMF) in the 'World Economic Outlook April 2010' confirms that the global economy is recovering at a much faster pace than previously expected. It adds that the pace of recovery is fairly slow in advanced countries but quite strong in developing and emerging economies. The US economy remains strong; in the developed region, the US has performed much better than its European counterparts and Japan. In the developing region, the emerging Asian countries are leading the process of recovery, the report adds. Expansive monetary policies provided the much-needed liquidity, and fiscal stimulus encouraged expenditures needed to pull the economy from a deep recession. How are the MENA countries faring? According to the IMF (2010), the MENA region is emerging from its downturn at a good speed. There are two main push factors. First, higher commodity prices and external demand are boosting production and exports in many economies in the region. Second, government spending programmes are playing a key role in fostering the recovery. In some economies, vulnerable financial sectors and weak property markets are holding it back (e.g. Kuwait, UAE).

GDP in the MENA grew by almost 4.5% in 2010, edging up to around 4.75% in 2011. Regarding the group of oil exporters, Qatar remains the strongest performer since the real activity is projected to expand by 18.5% in 2010. In Saudi Arabia and Kuwait, GDP grew at about 3.75% and 3% in 2010, respectively, supported in both cases by sizable government infrastructure investment. In the UAE, growth in 2010 was 1.25%, with property-related sectors expected to contract further. According to the IMF, Sub-Saharan Africa has weathered the global crisis well, and its recovery from the slowdown in 2009 was strong. Although some middle-income and oil-exporting economies were hit hard by the collapse in export and commodity markets, the region managed to avoid a contraction in 2009, growing by 2% in 2007. Its growth was projected to accelerate further.

The region's quick recovery reflects the relatively limited integration (implying muted impact) of most low-income economies into the global economy. The IMF offers a bullish outlook for the Indonesian economy, which grew by almost 6% in 2010 and a little more than 6% in 2011. The IMF notes an improving investment climate and sound management of fiscal and monetary policies in the country, believing that recent capital outflows from Indonesia are temporary and the European debt crisis poses a small downside risk to the country's growth. Attracted by the prospect of strong growth, investors have flocked to Indonesia's bond, stock and currency markets in the past year. There is also a massive increase in FDI. According the IMF, global economic growth reaches about 4.25% in 2010 and 2011. Advanced economies were expected to expand by 2.25% in 2010, and 2.5% in 2011, while emerging and developing economies were likely to grow by 6.25% during 2010–11.

There are risks, too. The room for policy adjustments in many advanced economies has been almost fully exhausted, and the economies, as a result, may not withstand new shocks. Risks related to the huge growth of public debt in developed countries have become very evident indeed. Market concerns about sovereign liquidity and solvency in Greece, if unchecked, could turn into a full-blown debt crisis. Such financial risks could be contagious and may depress output by prompting premature withdrawal of fiscal stimulus. The IMF stresses the need for 'rebalancing global demand' for sustained recovery. The countries having excessive external deficits before the crisis need to consolidate their public finance, and economies that ran excessive current account surpluses will need to further increase domestic demand. This will help sustain growth as high-deficit economies scale back their import demand. The surplus economies should appraise their currencies in order to rebalance export–import flows across countries. UN experts suggest that an early withdrawal of the fiscal and monetary stimulus packages from the major economies could cause the global economy to enter into a double-dip recession and an increase in public debt. This would be most severe in developed countries and recovery is likely to be slow. Such a recession would reduce government revenues even more, while further fall in GDP would continue to push up debt-to-GDP ratios and affect private sector confidence.

4. Globalization, Poverty and Islamic Countries

A World Bank Research Report (2002) suggests that globalization can reduce poverty:

> *'Globalization generally reduces poverty because more integrated economies tend to grow faster and this growth is usually widely diffused. As low-income countries break into global markets for manufactures and services, poor people can move from the vulnerability of grinding rural poverty to better jobs, often in towns or cities. In addition to this structural relocation, integration raises productivity job by job.'* [World Bank, *Globalization, Growth, and Poverty: Building an Inclusive World Economy* (World Bank Policy Research Report), January 2002, p. 1]

Joseph Stiglitz, an economics Nobel laureate in 2001, opined that rich countries can reduce world poverty by opening their protected markets (The World Bank Research Report, 2002, last cover page). Have Islamic countries benefited from globalization? Round (2007) shows that poverty in Africa has remained persistently high alongside a relatively slow globalizing process and generally sluggish growth performance. Page and Gelder (2002) suggest globalization was largely responsible for poverty reduction in MENA, which was an 'early integrator' into the global markets for capital and, especially, labour. The authors argued that international migration and official capital (aid) flows, driven largely by changes in the price of oil, were key factors in reducing poverty.

Globalization offers a window of opportunity for the Islamic world. The MENA is currently experiencing a 'youth bulge': it is estimated that 65% of the total population in the region is under the age of 30. Due to a lack of appropriate education and skills, youth unemployment is 25%, and about half of young unemployed people are first-time entrants into the job market. In comparison with 'Asian Tigers', the youth bulge could successfully exploit their human capital for generating growth (World Bank, 2007).

Is the GCC labour market biased? Foreign labour force participation in GCC countries is estimated to be around 75%, and for countries such as UAE and Qatar it can be as high as 95%. Most jobs are in the private sector and there is no well-defined policy on recruitment. Skilled foreigners (Asians) get priority over locals as they are obedient, prepared to work for lower wages, and come single. To cope with the challenges of globalization, the labour market should be improved by enforcing the right to form trades unions, collective bargaining, and more regulatory labour laws (Al-Najjar, 2006).

The World Bank Knowledge Economy Index (KEI) prepares to measure a country's preparedness to compete in today's knowledge economy. Of the countries of the OIC, the UAE tops the list; its latest (2008) position is 42 (amongst 140 countries included in the survey) and shows an improvement by 4 places over its 1995 ranking. Most Islamic countries have improved their knowledge base (most pronounced in the case of Oman) in the past decade, although Bahrain (due to significant weakening in the innovation pillar) and Lebanon suffered setbacks. Fast-growing China (ranked 77 and 97 in 2008 and 1995 respectively) and India (improved from 105 to 100 in the same period) registered marked progress in their knowledge base. Table 5 shows the top 10 Islamic countries in KEI.:

Table 1.5 Top 10 Islamic Countries (rank based on KEI 2008)

Countries	KEI 2008 (Rank)	KEI 1995 (Rank)
UAE	6.66 (42)	46
Qatar	6.15 (45)	50
Malaysia	6.06 (48)	48
Bahrain	6.02 (49)	35
Kuwait	6.01 (50)	52
Turkey	5.61 (53)	58
Jordan	5.53 (56)	63
Oman	5.37 (62)	72
Saudi Arabia	5.15 (65)	74
Lebanon	4.66 (70)	66

Source: World Bank, Knowledge Economy Index, Washington, DC.

Conclusion

There are 'winners' and 'losers' of globalization, leading to increasing frustration of the latter. Globalization should be managed in such a way that benefits are shared widely and costs are minimized. As the US financial crisis has shown, a local crisis can be translated into a full-scale global recession. Since the crisis, the Islamic financial and banking framework has become more prominent. Globalization, by offering a brighter future for all, provides perhaps the surest path to greater global security and world peace. Islamic countries (particularly oil-rich nations) have the potential to reap the full benefits of globalization. But it is necessary to diversify, as oil reserves will gradually be depleted; enhancing education, skills-formation and technological capabilities is of paramount importance for these countries. Incentives should be given for the efficient use of existing knowledge and the acquisition of new knowledge.

Life-long learning and continuing education programmes are expected to develop human capital further. Special attention should be given to higher education to scale up the knowledge base (e.g. by forging links with highly regarded foreign universities/institutions). Innovation, and the adoption of new technologies (incentives for R&D and scientific manpower) and ICT Infrastructure, and their application in the areas of e-learning and e-governance, are required to improve productivity.

In order to succeed in the wave of globalization, size does not matter. Singapore has proved that a small country can be successful. The GCC can provide much-needed leadership in various areas for the Islamic world (notably as a hub for education and training). According to the 2009 CPI (Corruption Perception Index), the existing governance structure is seemingly efficient and relatively 'clean': while Singapore is one of the least-corrupt countries in the world (Singapore ranks number 3, compared to Hong Kong 12, Japan/UK 17, and USA 19), the rankings of some Islamic countries are also noteworthy. For example, Qatar ranks 22 (above France, which ranks 24), the UAE ranks 30, Brunei/Oman 39, Bahrain 46, Jordan 49, Malaysia 56, Turkey 61, and Saudi Arabia 63. It is interesting to note that most Islamic countries are less corrupt than the fastest-growing emerging economies, such as China (79 on the 2009 CPI) and India (84).

It is imperative that Islamic countries should seize the benefits of globalization by establishing a knowledge-based economy, with the help of the ICT revolution.

References

Al-Najjar, B. (2006), 'Labor Migration to the GCC Countries', University of Bahrain, Unpublished.

Bannister, J. J. and Thugge, K. (2001), 'International Trade and Poverty Alleviation', *Finance and Development*, Vol. 38, No. 4, pp. 48–51.

ETH 2010, *KOF Index of Globalization 2010*, Zurich.

Hassan, M. K., Sanchez, B. A. and Hussain, M. E. (2010), 'Economic Performance of the OIC Countries and the Prospect of an Islamic Common Market', *Journal of Economic Cooperation and Development*, Vol. 31, No. 2, pp. 65–121.

INSEAD (2010), *Global Innovation Index Report 2009–10,* France.

International Monetary Fund (2009), *World Economic Outlook October 2009*, Washington, DC.

—. (2010), *World Economic Outlook April 2010*, Washington, DC.

—. (2010), *World Economic Outlook October 2010*, Washington, DC.

Noland, M. and Pack, H. (2004), 'Islam, Globalization, and Economic Performance in the Middle East', *SAIS Review*, Vol. 24, No. 2, pp. 105–116.

Johnson, D. G. (2002), 'Globalization: What it is and Who Benefits', *Journal of Asian Economics,* Vol. 13, No. 4, pp. 427–439.

Page, J. and Gelder, L. V. (2002), 'Globalization, Growth and Poverty Reduction in the Middle East and North Africa, 1970 -1999', Paper presented at the *Fourth Mediterranean Development Forum*, Amman, Jordan, 7–10 April.

Round, J. I. (2007), 'Globalization, Growth, Inequality and Poverty in Africa: A Macroeconomic Perspective', *UNU-WIDER Research Paper No. 2007/55*, Helsinki.

The Heritage Foundation (2010), *Index of Economic Freedom*, Washington, DC.

United Nations Development Programme (2009), *Human Development Report: Overcoming Barriers -- Human Mobility and Development*, New York.

World Bank (1998), *World Development Report: Knowledge for Development*, Oxford University Press: New York.

—. (2002), 'Globalization, Growth, and Poverty: Building an Inclusive World Economy', *World Bank Policy Research Report*, January 2002, Washington, DC.

—. (2007), 'Youth – An Undervalued Asset: Towards a New Agenda in the Middle East and North Africa. Progress, Challenges and Way Forward,' *World Bank Policy Note* No. 43372, Washington, DC.

—. (2010), *World Development Report: Development and Climate Change*, Washington, DC.
—. *Knowledge Economy Index* (various issues), Washington, DC.
World Economic Forum 2010, *Global Competitiveness Report 2010–11*, Geneva.

ECONOMIC INTEGRATION IN THE GCC: A LONG-TERM PERSPECTIVE

IKHLAAS GURRIB

Abstract

The research looks predominantly at the statistical harmonization among key macroeconomic variables such as GDP, Inflation Rates and Exchange Rates. For a single monetary variable across the GCC countries to work in the future, there is a need to test whether the different macroeconomic variables are compatible with each other in the long run. Co-integration testing can be performed through a framework such as the Johansen Co-integration test. This would provide key information for each country's policy makers on the implications of using a common currency. Findings suggest there is a long-run relationship between the top three GCC economies.

Keywords: Economic integration, GCC, Long run, Currency, Exchange Rates, Inflation

Introduction

> *'The events of recent months represent a historic change in the politics and governance of the MENA, and their effect is likely to be felt for years to come. Although most of the financial repercussions were initially limited to the countries at the epicenter of the political events, the oil-exporting countries were eventually affected as the unrest spread [...]. Overall, since early January stock markets have fallen sharply, and credit default swap spreads are much wider, although some markets have recovered from their worst levels. Citing heightened political risk, and in some cases, disruptions in real activity and fiscal weakening, rating agencies have undertaken numerous actions regarding several MENA countries, with Bahrain, Egypt, Jordan, Libya, and Tunisia among the countries downgraded. Financial links within the region – crossborder equity*

holdings as well as Bahrain's position as a regional banking hub – may lead to heightened regional transmission of shocks.' (IMF, 2011)

A clear point that emerges from the above quotation is that all the GCC countries are relatively closely related when it comes to the knock-on effects of events. In January 1999, eleven European currencies were locked to each other at fixed exchange rates. The successful move by the EU revitalized the efforts of the Gulf Cooperation Council (GCC) countries to push forward the long-awaited Gulf Monetary Union (GMU). The GCC objectives include coordination, integration and inter-connection between member states in all activity sectors, and formulation of similar regulations in economic and financial affairs, commerce, customs and communications.

Specifically, article 22 of the agreement reads: 'Member states shall seek to coordinate their financial, monetary and banking policies and enhance cooperation between monetary agencies and central banks, including the initiative to establish a joint currency in order to further their desired economic integration.' However, since the endorsement of the GCC Unified Economic Agreement (UEA) in 1981, which calls for a joint currency, the efforts towards a single currency in the Gulf have been slow. Nonetheless, at the Bahrain Summit, December 2000, leaders of the GCC sanctioned the agreement among GCC countries to multilaterally adopt the US dollar as the common currency peg. This initiative was taken to minimize the risk of exchange rates and stabilize exchange rates among GCC countries (BIS, 2010).

Important Assumptions about Monetary Union

The 1970 Werner Report on economic and monetary union in the European community states:

'*A monetary union implies inside its boundaries the total and irreversible convertibility of currencies, the elimination of margins of fluctuation in exchange rates, the irrevocable fixing of parity rates and the complete liberation of movements of capital.*' (The Werner Report, 1970)

Alternatively stated, three aspects should characterize a monetary union or a currency union. These are: (1) a single currency or several currencies that are fully convertible at an irrevocably fixed exchange rate; (2) union-wide monetary policy that is determined by a single central bank or a system of central banks; (3) a sole external exchange rate policy (Masson and Pattillo, 2001).

Fig. 2.1 Credit Default Swap Spread and Stock Market Performance of MENA Countries *(Basis points, 1 November 2010 – 17 March, 2011)*

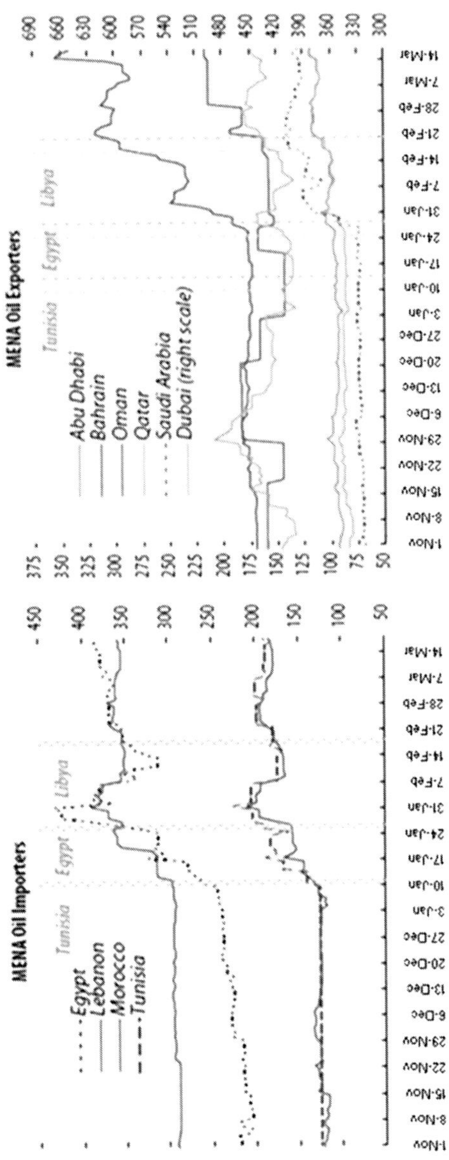

Fig. 2.1 Stock Markets Performance of MENA Countries *(Basis points, 1 November 2010 – 18 March, 2011)*

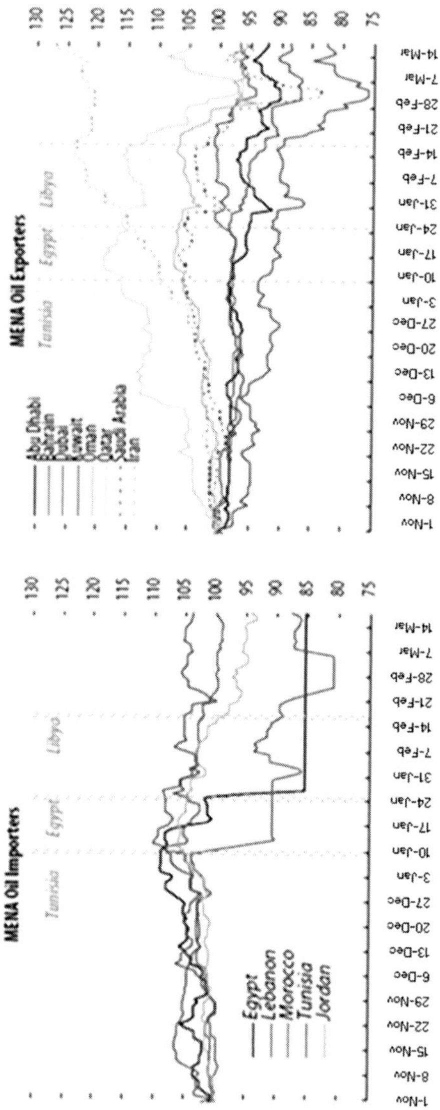

Sources: Bloomberg L.P.; and Markit
Note: MENA = Middle East and North Africa

The Need for a Monetary Union

Generally, ***benefits*** stem from the following:

1. The elimination of transaction and accounting costs. Most of these costs are associated with bid-ask spreads and commissions on foreign exchange transactions. For small and open economies with unsophisticated financial markets, direct savings in transactions after adopting a single currency are probably larger. Lowering transaction costs might lead to higher output and consumption gains.
2. The removal of foreign exchange risk, which is considered a major obstacle to trade and cross-border lending. It is argued that trade in goods and services, especially among small firms, will be enhanced, which would tend to intensify competition and increase allocative efficiency (Kenen, 1996). Rose (2000) contends that a common currency has a great positive effect on trade, and that the effect is much larger than the effect of reducing exchange-rate volatility to zero through an irrevocably fixed exchange rate arrangement (p.18).
3. A more transparent pricing system, making international price comparison easier. This also suggests that monetary union arrangements are less prone to speculative attacks (Frankel, 1999).
4. Obtaining a more credible monetary policy by adopting the strongest exchange-rate commitment (Frankel, 1999).

On the other hand, the ***costs*** of the process for adopting a single currency are mainly those involved in surrendering monetary autonomy. These costs are more likely to increase the more dissimilar the shocks for members' economic policies' tools are; namely the handling of the interest charge and of the exchange rate. Similarly, costs tend to increase the lower the flexibility of economic integration of country members, as a result of the difficulty of adjustment to shocks.

Common Features among the GCC Countries

The Gulf countries share several economic challenges, resulting in the need for the development of stronger economic integration. They collectively hold 40.2% of the world's proven oil reserves; they are leading oil producers, supplying 21.9% of the world's crude oil. Similarly, the GCC countries have at their disposal up to 23.4% of the world's natural gas reserves and account for 7.9% of the world's natural gas production.

The GCC countries enjoy relatively cheap oil- and gas-extraction costs, placing them in an advantageous position relative to other energy producers. The great wealth generated by the Gulf States allows their economies unprecedented development, with higher standards of living and modern physical infrastructure. The total GDP for GCC countries soared from $11 billion in 1971 to $821 billion in 2007. The total GCC population increased by 43.5% in the years 2005 to 2010.

Business Cycle Harmonization

The synchronization of member countries' business cycles is probably one of the least contentious criteria in the literature for joining a monetary union. Countries with highly correlated business cycles tend to have a higher propensity to join a monetary union, for their responses to shocks tend to be similar too. If shocks hit member countries asymmetrically, policy responses will differ across countries. And if those countries are members of a monetary union, then the common monetary policy cannot serve simultaneously the stabilization of the economy for each member country.

The GCC economies are characterized by being highly oil-based, and hence they are subject to similar shocks originating from oil market developments. The correlation coefficients of GDP growth rates in the GCC are quite mixed: Qatar has relatively high coefficients in comparison with the other five countries.[1] (Table 1)

The correlation coefficients tend to decrease further when they are calculated for different sample periods (i.e. the 1980s and the 1990s), probably for two reasons: (1) the strong influence of the sharp increase of oil prices in the 1970s relative to the 80s and 90s; (2) the greater differences in recent years between GCC economies. This suggests the need to cross-check for any long-term relationships following changes in macroeconomic variables.

[1] Note that the available data for Bahrain's GDP start only in 1980 in the World Bank database (2011) and the United Nations Database (2011). Bahrain data is discarded in later analysis as the scope of this study being limited to the top 3 GCC nations.

Table 2.1 Correlation Coefficients of Output Growth (1974–2009)

	Bahrain	Kuwait	Oman	SA	UAE	Qatar
Bahrain	1.00					
Kuwait	0.37	1.00				
Oman	0.77	0.38	1.00			
SA	-0.09	0.12	-0.06	1.00		
UAE	0.86	0.45	0.81	0.11	1.00	
Qatar	0.81	0.52	0.73	0.12	0.91	1.00

Source: World Bank Database and United Nations Statistics Division. GDP at 2002 dollar prices.

Literature Review

A number of studies have tried to determine whether the GCC countries are ready to establish a monetary union based on their market economies. Laabas and Limam (2002), for example, used a formal test based on the generalized purchasing power parity and found that GCC countries had not yet met the pre-requirements to establish a monetary union, due to the fact that the GCC economies were oil-dependent, had little intra-trade, lacked convergence in macroeconomic fundamentals, and lacked synchronization in business cycles. They concluded that establishing a monetary union might align the business cycles, thus increasing intra-trade among the GCC countries.

Jadresic (2002) concluded that launching a common currency for the GCC countries would bring about many benefits, yet it would not be enough for successful economic integration. Removal of domestic and cross-border distortions that hinder trade and investments, coordinating policies, and increasing political alliances are steps that should be taken in order to achieve successful integration. By testing for co-integration among the GCC countries' GDPs, inflation rates, exchange rates and monetary bases, Darrat and Al-Shamsi (2005) concluded that the GCC countries are compatible to establish a monetary union. Nonetheless, the failure in doing so is due to socio-political factors that have hampered the process towards the monetary union. A more recent study by Louis, Rosmy and Mohammad (2008) tested whether the GCC countries are subject to symmetric aggregate demand (AD) and non-oil aggregate supply (AS) shocks. Their results were that GCC countries' AD shocks were symmetrical with the US, but their non-oil AS shocks were not. These findings support the use of the US dollar as a common anchor for the GCC countries since US monetary policy can help smooth demand shocks in these countries. A study by Abu-Bader and Abu-Qarn (2006) concluded that the GCC countries were not yet ready to establish a monetary union. The authors used three different methods to test the GCC economies. The first method was the Structural VAR to identify both demand and supply shocks, and to analyse whether these shocks were symmetrical or not. The second method was the use of co-integration tests to find whether long-term relationships of real GDP among all the possible paired countries existed. The third method was to determine whether there were common business cycles among the GCC countries. None of the three methods provided support for establishing a monetary union.

Stable exchange rates

Recently, the GCC countries have realized the significant importance of the US dollar for their foreign trade, in which transactions are settled mainly in US dollars. In particular, the GCC's oil revenue represents the largest part of its revenues (Table 5). It is also worth mentioning that petroleum activities account for a large proportion of GDP. In 2007, on average, petroleum activities represented 45.7% of GDP among the GCC countries (Table 2). Consequently, they pegged their national currencies to the US dollar. Alternatively stated, the GCC currencies have demonstrated a history of synchronized exchange rate movements against the US dollar and stable cross-exchange rates. In the 1970s all were revalued by as much as 14% to 18%, with the exception of the Omani riyal (OR), which took a reverse trend and was devalued by 9%. Although to a lesser extent, in the 1980s the Bahraini dinar (BD), Qatar riyal (QR) and Emirate dirham (ED) were revalued again, and the other three were devalued by as much as 11% for both the Saudi riyal (SR) and the OR, and by about 7% for the Kuwaiti dinar (KD). In the 1990s, the BD, QR, SR and ED were virtually stable, neither devalued nor revalued. The KD and the OR ended the decade with a devaluation of 6% and a revaluation of 8% respectively.

Table 2.2 GCC Petroleum Industry share of GDP (%)

	Bahrain	Kuwait	Oman	SA	UAE	Qatar
2003	18.3	45.8	40.9	31.3	28.4	57.6
2004	18.5	44.7	42.2	31.8	31.9	54.5
2005	15.6	45.2	48.7	31.9	35.7	54.4
2006	14.5	44.2	47.6	30.7	38.1	52.5
2007	13.5	41.4	44.3	28.8	38.6	51.0
2008	12.8	46.2	50.6	28.9	38.8	50.1
2009	13.3	48.6	40.6	26.6	39.2	49.6

Sources: Central Banks of each country. GDP at constant 2000 prices

In general, all the six currencies have emerged from a period of large adjustments, particularly in the 1970s, which was considered a new phase of development following the unexpected changes in the international oil market. However, the currencies' volatility diminished during the second half of the 1980s and the 1990s. Policy makers in the GCC are aware of the risk of devaluation, particularly the possibility of provoking unexpected detrimental results. They are also aware that if devaluation is used once, it will be more difficult to use it again in the future.

Similarly, when devaluations are used systematically, they will lead to more inflation with no gains in output (De Grauwe, 1994). Nevertheless, this should not give the impression that the exchange rate mechanism should be discarded, for it can be used effectively. The conclusion of the analysis was to ask what the motivation for the adoption of a single currency would be, as long as the exchange rate risk was virtually nonexistent. One argument is that a single currency may promote trade if the effects of exchange rate risk are significant. It seems that all GCC currencies have managed to maintain the credibility of their fixed exchange arrangements by avoiding the devaluation option, even in periods of very real depressed oil prices (latter part of the 1990s).

The importance of economic convergence

Proponents of the convergence approach stress the need for nominal convergence to reduce the costs of losing monetary policy independence. Although failing to achieve convergence may not prevent attaining the ultimate goal of a monetary union, it would definitely make the way to the union harder (Crockett, 1994). The debate was carried on between two groups, known as the 'economists' and the 'monetarists'. The economists argue that national economies of member countries should converge before launching a single currency and proceeding to deeper economic integration. They argue that even if nominal exchange rates are fixed, real exchange rates will not be permanently fixed unless member countries achieve common rates of inflation. The economic rationale behind this is that if members of the block have different levels of economic performance, fixing exchange rates would force high-inflation countries to carry out deflationary measures, which would aggravate regional disparities within the union. They therefore view as an essential step the coordination and *harmonization* of macroeconomic policies, through a high degree of economic performance convergence, prior to a monetary union (Pilbeam, 1992).

The monetarists, on the other hand, assert that the union itself would produce convergence. In their view, convergence would be achieved through exchange rate commitments, which could be implemented without *ex ante* convergence. They doubt the notion that countries will make the effort to coordinate their monetary policies without fixing exchange rates (Pilbeam, 1992). This research aims to support the economists by testing the effect of a single currency prior to the introduction of monetary union.

Importance of prerequisite nominal criteria

The *significance of prerequisite nominal criteria* stems from the fact that they are likely to make progress towards monetary union smoother, but not trouble free. They also have the advantage of making national policy makers more disciplined by the time they come under one monetary authority. It is important therefore that the GCC members agree on a number of nominal criteria that suit their economies and address their specificity. Convergence would lead to a reduction of differences between national goals, such as the reduction of differences between national debt ratios.

Convergence in fiscal deficits and debts, both of which are necessary for stable monetary unions, is of paramount importance for the Gulf. These preconditions for convergence could be viewed as a screening device aimed at keeping out members that might be reluctant to adopt prudent macroeconomic policies once they were full members of the union. The introduction of convergence was intended to create a monetary union with a future of low inflation, and to move the focus of macroeconomic policies implemented by member countries from the domestic level to that of monetary union (Bayoumi and Mauro, 2001).

EMU: An example of convergence criteria

The Maastricht Treaty (1991) established the Maastricht criteria. The four numerical convergence criteria involve targets on the convergence of inflation, interest rates, exchange rates and government debt and deficits (Bayoumi and Mauro, 2001). According to the Treaty, member countries are obliged to attain a rate of consumer price inflation within 1.5% of the average of the three best-performing countries during the year prior to entering the EMU. By developing an inflation convergence criterion, the union would be more likely to become a low-inflation zone. The second criterion of long-term interest rates is strongly connected to expected inflation. The long-term interest rates in a national currency reflect both the global real interest rate and a currency-specific premium or discount, on which expected inflation differentials are the most affecting factor.

For an EMU member to be ready to enter stage three, its long-term interest rates should be confined within two percentage points of the average rates prevailing in the three countries with the best inflation record (Crockett, 1994). The primary aim of requiring a convergence of inflation rates and interest rates is to avoid large real exchange rate changes once nominal rates are locked (Bayoumi and Mauro, 2001).

In line with the Maastricht Treaty, this study will look at the issue of currency convergence initially, by setting threshold currency convergence criteria.

2. Research Methodology and Data

Research Hypotheses

H_1: There are no significant *long run* economic relationships among the top three GCC member countries' currencies.

H_2: There are significant *long run* economic relationships among the top three GCC member countries' currencies.

The above hypotheses test whether there is any existing statistical harmonization among the top three GCC countries. Lack of long run relationships would suggest a need to reevaluate how GCC macroeconomic policies should be implemented, in coordination with each other, in order to achieve a workable monetary union.

Econometric models for long run relationships: Testing for cointegration as a means of measuring the degree of integration (or segmentation) among markets in the same country or across countries and regions has become quite popular in recent applied economics and finance literature. Examples include Bowe and Mylanidis (1999), Phylaktis (1999), and Ghosh and al. (1999). To the author's knowledge, only Darrat and Shamsi (2003) and Abu-Bader and Abu-Qarn (2006) have been using cointegration approaches to test for long run relationships. The specifications of the long run dynamics models can be found in Gurrib (2011).

Conversion Rate of the new Gulf currency

Conversion rates will serve as the base for converting all money-related and cash balances as well as for the exchange of old banknotes for new ones. This approach requires a division of the six currencies into two groups based on their current official exchange rates denominated in US dollars. Group 1 includes the currencies whose current exchange values are multiples of dollars (BD, KD and OR); Group 2 includes the currencies whose current values are fractions of the US dollar (QR, SR, ED). Thereafter, the calculated median of each group is used as a base for the new currency conversion rate. The aim is to bring the value of the two groups of currencies as close as possible to the new currency, by setting the new currency equal to (1/x) of Group 1 currencies (e.g. one-tenth) and at par with Group 2 currencies. This is illustrated in Table 3.

Table 2.3 GCC New Currency rate

	Currency	USD per local currency	Median	New Currency	Deviation from new currency	
					Value	%
Group 1	Bahrain	2.6440			-0.0390	-1.48%
	Kuwait	3.4172	2.6440		0.7342	21.49%
	Oman	2.5910			-0.0920	-3.55%
				0.2683		
Group 2	SA	0.2665			-0.0018	-0.68%
	UAE	0.2722	0.2722		0.0039	1.43%
	Qatar	0.2744			0.0061	2.22%

Note: New currency is calculated as the average of 0.1*Group 1 median + Group 2 median. Currencies pegged to the US dollar for July 2000 to June 2011.

As shown in the last column of Table 3, all the six currencies require certain official actions, revaluation or devaluation, to bring them into parity with the new currency, which equals $0.2683. With the exception of the KD, none of the currencies calls for a value change of more than 3.55% in absolute value. According to this method, the BD, OR and SR require revaluations by 1.48%, 3.55% and 0.68% respectively. On the other hand, the KD, QR and ED require devaluations of 23.8%, 2.0% and 1.2% respectively. Since the KD is the only currency whose difference from the new currency exceeds 20%, it could be dealt with as a special case.

In this situation, the cross-exchange rate of the KD could be used as a new currency relative to the US dollar. For instance, if the KD = US $3.4172 and the new currency = US $0.2683, the cross-exchange rate of new currency/KD should be 12.736. Broadly speaking, this method has the benefit of creating easier conversion rates that facilitate the transition to the new currency.

However, its disadvantage is the need for abrupt changes to the official exchange rates (revaluation or devaluation). Revaluation would increase the real value of public debts and decrease the relative price of traded to non-traded goods. Devaluation might disrupt the process towards meeting convergence criteria, especially inflation, given the GCC's high degree of dependence on imports.

It is hard to get convergence of inflation rates and devaluations simultaneously. But since none of the GCC economies has a history of high inflation except during 2004–2008, which could be viewed as an exceptional period, and with the absence of flexible wages, going through devaluation would not be likely to create unmanageable problems. Nonetheless, it would be better if the devaluation of exchange rates was carried out as the very last step, immediately before the old national currencies were replaced by the single currency, when the credibility of national currencies was no longer an issue (Giovannini, 1991).

Robustness of the New Currency Rate

So far, the methodology used has resulted in a New Currency of \$0.2683, which has led to a devaluation of the KD by over 20%. As mentioned earlier, devaluation might cause noise in attaining a harmonized currency union. From Table 1, it can be seen that the noise would be roughly 19.44% (16.46% from Group 1 and 2.98% from Group 2).

To reduce these possible devaluations and revaluations, the new currency can be set as any of the currency values. The above method is robust, tested by substituting each currency as the New GCC Currency, and testing whether it works towards a better harmonized currency, i.e. results in fewer disruptions in the net GCC current currency values.

The above method can be further modified since KD needs a devaluation of 23.8 against the New Currency. For instance, due to the relatively higher GDP of SA and the highest likelihood of SA hosting the most lucrative regional financial centre, all other currencies can be revalued or devalued against the new currency (SAR), keeping SAR fixed at 0.2667. While not all results are reported here, the use of the Qatari currency as the New GCC currency produced the least disturbance for the other 5 countries. This is illustrated in Table 4.

Table 2.4 Benchmarking the Qatar Dinar as the New Currency rate

	Currency	USD per local currency	Median	New Currency	Deviation from new currency		Net Noise
					Value	%	
Group 1	Bahrain	2.6440			-0.1000	-3.78%	
	Kuwait	3.4172	2.6440		0.6732	19.70%	
	Oman	2.5910			-0.1530	-5.91%	10.01%
				0.2744			
Group 2	SA	0.2665			-0.0079	-2.96%	
	UAE	0.2722	0.2722		0.0022	-0.81%	
	Qatar	0.2744			0.0000	0.00%	-3.77%
							6.24%

Note: New currency is calculated as the average of 0.1*Group1 median + Group2 median. Currencies pegged to the US dollar for July 2000 to June 2011.

The effect of using the QD as the new currency on other countries' interest rates and inflation rates can also be tested using IRF. This study fills the gap by looking at the long-term dynamics that exist among the key macroeconomic variables in the top three GCC member countries, using a quarter window covering data from 1 July 2000 to 30 June 2011. The scope of this study is to look at the currency convergence and analyse the effect of the common new currency on each of the top three member countries' two key macroeconomic variables, namely their GDP and inflation rates.

Key data were obtained from the Central Banks of each country, and cross-checked against reports from the Bank of International Settlements (BIS), the World Bank and the United Nations Databases. To standardize the available data, all data were set using 2002 constant prices.

3. Research Findings

Long-term relationships

Prior to establishing a regression for any econometric model under study, all the series were tested using the Augmented Dickey Fuller (ADF) unit root test. To ensure lag optimization, without losing too much of economic significance, the Schwarz Information Criteria were used. All individual series appeared to be stationary at 1%, 5% and 10% significance levels. To test whether the different currencies shared any long run relationships, the Johansen Cointegration test was carried out, the results for which are presented in Table 5.

Table 2.5 Testing of Long run Relationships among the three currencies

Trace Test			
Hypothesized No. of CE (s)	Eigenvalue	Trace Statistic	Critical Value
None*	0.461	43.79078	29.79707
At most 1*	0.250	17.84031	15.49471
At most 2*	0.128	5.760544	3.841466
Eigenvalue test			
Hypothesized No. of CE (s)	Eigenvalue	Max-Eigen Statistic	Critical Value
None*	0.461	25.95047	21.13162
At most 1*	0.250	12.07977	14.2646
At most 2*	0.128	5.760544	3.841466

* denotes rejection of the hypothesis at the 0.05 level

Findings from the trace test suggest there are 3 cointegration equations at the 5% significance level, while the max-eigenvalue test indicates 1 cointegration equation. Both results support the existence of a long run relationship between the three major currencies in the Middle East.

Concluding Remarks

Convergence with regard to various preconditions is a good step towards a harmonized GCC. However, convergence of some macroeconomic indicators would not solve every problem of the GCC economies. Launching structural changes that address particular economic conditions of the GCC would be vital as well. The economies of the GCC are at a different stage of development from those of countries belonging to the EMU and therefore have different challenges. Problems manifested in the GCC include the unemployment rates, and the lack of diversified economies. But 'how much nominal convergence needs to be established before launching the single currency?' is a hard question to answer. This is a policy matter demanding a multilateral agreement, since it involves sacrifices that member countries will have to go through. This paper also demonstrates the difficulty of having a single currency caused by the conflict between revaluations/devaluations and inflation. The use of the QR seems to work best in producing the fewest revaluations/devaluations.

In line with this study, future research could include models for short run dynamics where the effect of the adoption of the new currency was tested. As a starting point, it would be essential to work out the standard deviation of the new currency for each of the three countries' currencies.

References

Abu-Bader, Suleiman and Abu-Qarn, Aamer (2006). 'On the Optimality of a GCC Monetary Union: Structural VRA, Common Trends and Common Cycles Evidence' (Ben-Gurion University of the Negev).

Abu-Bader, Suleiman and Abu-Qarn, Aamer (2010). 'Irving Fisher Committee on Central Bank Statistics'. Bank of International Settlements, IFC Bulletin N° 32, pp. 23–58. Retrieved from: http://www.bis.org/ifc/publ/ifcb32.pdf [Accessed on 03/01/2011].

Bowe, M., and N. Mylonidis (1999). 'Is the European Capital Market Ready for the Single Currency?', Journal of Business Finance and Accounting, 26: 1–32.

Crockett, Andrew (1994). 'The role of convergence in the process of EMU' in Alfred Steinherr '30 Years of European Monetary Integration From the Werner Plan to EMU'. Longman, New York.

Darrat, Ali; Al-Shamsi, Fatima (2003). 'On the Path to Integration in the Gulf Region: Are the Gulf Economies Sufficiently Compatible?'.

De Grauwe, Paul (1994). 'The Economics of Economic Integration', Oxford University Press.

Frankel, Jeffrey (1999). 'No Single Currency Regime Is Right For All Countries Or At All Times'. Essays in International Finance, No. 215, August, Princeton University, New Jersey.

Ghosh, A., R. Saidi, and K. H. Johnson (1999). 'Who Moves the Asian-Pacific Stock Markets-U.S. or Japan?' The Financial Review, 34: 159–170.

Gurrib, I. (2011) 'Does the Money Endogeneity Theory of Post-Keynesian Economics apply in Frontier Emerging Markets? The case of Saudi Arabia'. International Journal of Finance and Management, Volume 1, Issue 1, pp. 21–31, London, UK.

IMF. 'Durable Financial Stability: Getting There from Here', World Economic and Financial Surveys, Global Financial Stability Report, April, 2011. Retrieved from:http://www.imf.org/external/pubs/ft/gfsr/2011/01/pdf/text.pdf [Accessed on 06/06/2011]

Jadresic, Esteban (2002). 'On a Common Currency for the GCC Countries', IMF Policy Discussion Paper.

Kenen, Peter B. (1996). 'Making EMU Happen – Problems and Proposals: A Symposium', Princeton University, August 1996, Princeton, New Jersey.

Laabas, Belkacem and Imed Limam (2002). 'Are GCC Countries Ready for Currency Union?' (Arab Planning Institute- Kuwait), 2002.

Louis, Balli, and Osman (2008). 'Monetary Union among Arab Gulf Cooperation Council (AGCC) Countries: Does the symmetry of shocks extend to the non-oil sector?' Munich Personal RePEc Archive, 2008.

Maastricht Treaty. Economic and Monetary Union, 1991. Retrieved from: http://europa.eu/legislation_summaries/economic_and_monetary_affairs/institutional_and_economic_framework/treaties_maastricht_en.htm . [Accessed on 05/02/2011]

Masson, Paul and Catherine Pattillo (2001). 'Monetary Union in West Africa (ECOWAS): Is It Desirable and How Could It Be Achieved?' IMF Occasional Paper, 2001.

Phylaktis, K. (1999). 'Capital Market Integration in the Pacific Basin Region: An Impulse Response Analysis'. Journal of International Money and Finance, 18, 267–287, 1999.

Pilbeam, Keith (1992). 'International Finance'. Macmillan, London.

Rose, Andrew (2000). 'One money, one market: the effect of common currencies on trade' Economic Policy, No 30, pp. 9–45.

Tamim Bayoumi & Paolo Mauro (2001). 'The Suitability of ASEAN for a Regional Currency Arrangement'. The World Economy, Wiley Blackwell, vol. 24(7), pp. 933–54.

United Nations Statistics Division. Data Series. 2011. Retrieved from: http://data.un.org/Search.aspx?q=GDP. [Accessed on 12/11/2010]

Werner Report of 1970 in Alfred Steinherr '30 Years of European Monetary Integration From the Werner Plan to EMU'. Longman, New York, 1994.

World Bank Indicators. 2011. http://data.worldbank.org/indicator/NY.GDP.MKTP.CD?page=5. [Accessed on 15/01/2011].

EFFECTIVE LEADERSHIP BEHAVIOURS AMONG THE PRESIDENTS OF PUBLIC UNIVERSITIES: COMPARISON OF FRANCE AND IRAN

DOMINIQUE BESSON AND DANIELLE KHALIFE

Abstract

Higher education is of great significance in every society because it influences all aspects of life, including technology, culture, science, economy, industry, agriculture, and even politics. In this paper, we will consider universities as organizations and try to evaluate effective leadership methods in these organizations. Our main objective is to identify the extent to which effective leadership behaviours are used by university Presidents, and to compare Iranian and French universities in this regard.

Keywords: Leadership, higher education, behaviour, France, Iran.

Introduction

Higher education is of great significance because it influences all aspects of society, including technology, culture, science, economy, industry, agriculture, and even politics. The ultimate outcome of the whole education system, from elementary school onwards, becomes evident when individuals graduate from higher education. The growth and development of a country depend on how well developed its universities and research activities are.

Great advances in technology and changes in the global economy have led to a situation in which young people need more formal education (Center for Educational Research and Innovation, 1982; Allen, 1988; Paytas, Gradeck and Andrews, 2004).

Higher education and its management are rooted in the social, cultural, political, organizational and economic history of a country or nation. Nowadays there is a widespread belief worldwide that this field of management requires national, regional and international reform. Usually, however, no inherent mechanism can be found in institutions of higher education to respond to this need for change; therefore, careful scientific planning is required for these reforms.

Although some people treat the terms 'management' and 'leadership' as synonyms, the two should be distinguished. There has always been debate on the differences between a leader and a manager. Bennis and Nanus (1985), for example, believe that the managers are those who do things right, but the leaders are those who do right things; i.e. the most important thing for a manager is the result, but a leader also focuses on how that result is achieved. Zaleznik (1977) says that managers are concerned with how work is carried out, while leaders focus on the meaning of the work among the workers.

However, Yukl (1994) believes that it is not impossible for a person to be a manager and a leader at the same time. There are various leadership and management approaches within different types of organizations. In educational organizations, especially universities, various cultures and processes exist that distinguish them from other organizations and require different leadership and managerial approaches.

Although leadership in universities has not been extensively studied, several researchers have tried to study leadership approaches in organizations in general.

One aspect that makes studying leadership in higher education difficult, ambiguous and complicated is the diversity of definitions of both leadership and higher education. Stogdill (1974) concluded that the number of definitions provided for leadership almost matches the number of individuals who have tried to define it. This problem has resulted in a lack of good studies on organizational leadership in general and for the university sector in particular.

One of the problems concerning leadership research in higher education organizations is that the organizational characteristics of universities and other HE institutions are so different from those of other types of organizations that conventional management theories cannot easily be applied to them.

Many senior academic administrators have trained primarily for academic careers (teaching, research, etc.) and have rarely had management training. When they move into senior leadership positions, both academic and administrative staff, with years of academic experience, realize that they must quickly develop the new and different knowledge and skills needed to manage an institution. This can cause serious problems in leadership of higher education institutions, especially in the face of a constantly changing environment (McDade, 1988).

The concept of leadership and its dimensions have evolved through the literature, and the cultural context has been considered as a variable in analysing leadership styles within specific contexts. In fact, leadership practices differ according to context (the specific region or country; the type of organization). Therefore, leadership practices are expressed through cultural perspectives (Kouzes and Posner, 2003). So when studying leadership behaviours, we have to know these specific contexts and their implications for the practice of leadership.

In this research, we considered the context in which Iranian and French higher education leaders perform, and its impacts on how they actually work. French higher education underwent a substantial reform recently, *'la loi relative aux libertés et responsabilités des universités'* (LRU), and there is still much debate about its positive and negative aspects. In light of these reforms, leadership seems to have gained more importance, as more autonomy and power are delegated to the university Presidents. In countries like Iran, with a centralized educational system, universities are more dependent on governments.

In general, universities are considered as organizations that try to evaluate the effectiveness of their own leadership methods. Our main objective is to identify the extent to which effective leadership behaviours are used by university Presidents, comparing Iranian and French universities. We first present our main issue and the purpose of our study, then the methodology we used. We then present our results, and finally give extensive, even synthetic, discussion of the results, including some limitations of this work.

1. Question research: the five effective leadership behaviours of University Presidents

This research is based on the leadership study approach proposed by Jim Kouzes and Barry Posner (1983), who tried to look deeply into the leader–subordinate relationship. After studying and analysing the responses they received from successful leaders, Kouzes and Posner found that most of the success stories had features in common. They identified a number of practices that were common in all extraordinary leadership achievements and called them the Five Practices of Exemplary Leadership. The practices are:

Model the Way: The most important personal quality people look for and admire in a leader is personal credibility. Leaders model the way by finding their voice and setting an example. Modelling the way begins with the clarification of personal values and involves building and affirming shared values that all can embrace.

Inspire a Shared Vision: Leaders are driven by their clear image of possibility and what their organization could become. Leaders inspire a shared vision by envisioning the future and enlisting others in a common vision. They cannot command commitment; they can only inspire it. On the other hand, in order to be loyal to their leader, subordinates must believe that leaders understand their needs and have their interests at heart.

Challenge the Process: No leader can be effective if he/she intends to keep things the same. Leaders challenge the process by searching for opportunities and by experimenting, taking risks, and learning from mistakes. They are early supporters and adopters of innovation. However, change can be stressful, so leaders must also create a climate in which people are psychologically ready.

Enable Others to Act: Leaders know that they cannot do everything alone. Leadership is a team effort. Leaders enable others to act by fostering collaboration and supporting others. Since cooperation requires trust, leaders help create a trusting climate in which subordinates are involved and feel important.

Encourage the Heart: Since success is almost always hard to achieve, people are often tempted to give up. Leaders encourage the heart by recognizing contributions and celebrating values and victories. By paying attention, offering encouragement, personalizing appreciation, and maintaining a positive outlook, leaders stimulate, rekindle and focus people's energies.

This approach is a comprehensive, and yet simplified, approach to leadership. Since it is based on a quantitative scoring system – which has been extensively studied and validated in the literature – it can be easily used to quantify leadership behaviours. This is especially useful when a comparative study, such as the present research, is undertaken. In addition, we used the Leadership Practices Inventory (LPI), a questionnaire used to measure effective leadership behaviours in Kouzes and Posner's theory, one of the latest questionnaires for leadership evaluation. It can be used to measure effective leadership behaviours, as well as transactional and transformational leadership ones. Using 'Self' and 'Others' versions, we can demonstrate the differences between the opinions of managers and those of their co-workers. Using a simple tool to evaluate the characteristics and effective leadership behaviours of university Presidents in France and Iran may demonstrate the influences of their respective situations on the leaders' behaviours. Furthermore, studying leadership methods and behaviours in developing countries such as Iran in comparison with those in developed countries such as France can yield interesting results. In the case of France, especially after the LRU reforms and the increased power given to university Presidents, it is interesting to see how Kouzes and Posner's five effective leadership behaviours can help improve universities there. Applying the same approach to Iran is interesting for two reasons. First, to see to what extent Presidents in a centralized university system might be engaged in these five behaviours; and second, it is good to compare Iranian features as a centralized university system with France as a decentralized system. Leadership effectiveness can be defined in many ways, using such criteria as goal achievement, flexible management, resource increase, or stake-holder satisfaction. Being effective in one aspect of organizational performance may prevent effectiveness in other aspects of performance. Universities, since they are generally financed using public money, solely or in addition to private resources, come under extreme pressure from governments to enhance their performance outcomes. The aim of this study is to find out whether current higher education leadership in Iran and France is effective, and if not, to what factors this failure can be attributed, and what can be done to improve the situation.

2. Methodology

Our objective in this study was to see what behaviours university Presidents demonstrate in order to lead their organizations effectively. In this regard, we compared French and Iranian university Presidents.

Differences in culture, personality and contexts can deeply influence leadership method and effectiveness. Iran and France are two countries with different cultural, social, public and historical backgrounds. In particular, there are procedures and protocols for the selection of university Presidents. In France, they are elected mainly by the faculty (decentralized procedure), while in Iran, Presidents are appointed by the Ministry of Science, Research and Technology (centralized procedure).

Study Population

Given the great variety of higher education institutions in France (public, private, online, or Schools of Business) and in Iran (public, private, or online institutes), we decided to focus exclusively on public universities in both Iran and France. In Iran, this study included all public universities that are affiliated to the Ministry of Science, Research and Technology. All university Presidents and 4 or 5 Vice Presidents in each university were included, and each received our questionnaire. In France likewise, all public universities were included; and all university Presidents and 4 or 5 Vice Presidents in each university received our questionnaire.

Structure of the questionnaire

We used Kouzes and Posner's LPI as our data gathering tool. The LPI consisted of 30 statements that address the essential behaviours found when people report being at their personal best as leaders. In addition to a 'Self' version, the 'Others' version allows for comprehensive feedback from electors, managers, colleagues and others in order to provide a balanced picture of leadership behaviours and constructive discussion of ways to improve. The LPI comprises 6 statements for each of the 5 practices of exemplary leadership:

- Statements 1, 6, 11, 16, 21 and 26 measure 'Model the way' behaviour:
- Statements 2, 7, 12, 17, 22 and 27 measure 'Inspire a shared vision' behaviour;
- Statements 3, 8, 13, 18, 23 and 28 measure 'Challenge the process' behaviour;
- Statements 4, 9, 14, 19, 24 and 29 measure 'Enable others to act' behaviour;
- Statements 5, 10, 15, 20, 25 and 30 measure 'Encourage the heart' behaviour.

Computerized scoring software provides feedback along a number of dimensions, including comparisons by respondent category or relationship with the normative database, rankings by frequency, and variances between 'Self' and 'Observer' scores. In order to cover other areas of interest, we added 7 open-ended questions for both countries, and an 8th one for France concerning specifically the LRU.

- Q1: What are the positive aspects of leadership in your institution?
- Q2: What are the negative aspects of leadership in your institution?
- Q3: What would you recommend to improve the current leadership?
- Q4: How do managers and leading academic staff in your institution work?
- Q5: Have the management system or formal rules changed in recent years in your institution? If yes, please describe the changes. Do you consider this an improvement?
- Q6: Has leadership changed in your institution in recent years? If yes, please describe the changes. Do you consider this an improvement?
- Q7: Have you recently witnessed conflicts because of the leadership in your institution? If yes, could you describe them?
- Q8: Do you think the recent legal changes (LRU for example) will significantly change the leadership behaviours of university Presidents? If yes, how?

After reviewing all answers to each open-ended question, we classified them into a number of categories; i.e. responses that delivered a similar opinion were gathered in a group. This process was carried out by the researcher and confirmed by an independent reviewer.

Translation – Reverse translation – Pilot study

LPI, like most other survey tools, originated in North America and is in English. We took the same steps as those mentioned by Besson and Haddaj (2005) to evaluate the accuracy of the translation of the LPI into French and Farsi. We used the reverse translation method, which seems to be the most cumbersome to implement, but also clearly the most reliable. In this method, the text is translated from the original to the desired language, and then it is translated back, by different people, to the original language in order to see how similar it is to the original version.

Data collection

In Iran, the questionnaires were distributed by mail or in person to the university Presidents and Vice Presidents. In France, we sent the electronic version of the questionnaire through a 'Survey Monkey' website. Confidentiality of responses was maintained for respondents in both countries.

3. Data Analysis

The data obtained were analysed statistically using software SPSS 11.5, and were categorized as either descriptive or deductive. In the descriptive part of the analysis, the number of subjects in Iran and France and their statistical measures (such as mean and standard deviation) were compared with each other; tables and graphs were used to demonstrate these variables. In the deductive part, independent T-test and Two-Way Analysis of Variance (ANOVA) were used to answer the study questions.

Another useful and informative way to analyse our data was to compare the scores given by university Presidents and Vice Presidents in Iran and France with the average score among all respondents to the LPI questionnaire worldwide. A database has been established by a consultative company, Fine Points Professionals Ltd., – which is affiliated to John Wiley & Sons Inc., the publisher of The Leadership Challenge materials and the LPI – as The Leadership Challenge® Authorized Service Center. This database includes the responses that have been given by all respondents from all types of organization in any country that has used this questionnaire. We used the services provided by Fine Points Professionals Ltd. to determine the percentile of French and Iranian university Presidents' scores in the five effective leadership behaviours in comparison with the general score of all respondents to the LPI questionnaire. The results are shown in Table 3.1.

Results

The total number of subjects was 179, of which 72 were Iranian and 107 were French. Of the 72 Iranian subjects, 20 were Presidents and 52 VPs; among the 107 French, 10 were Presidents and 97 VPs. Table 3.1. shows the mean score and standard deviation of each questionnaire item (leadership behaviour) based on the President and VP groups in Iran and France.

Table 3.1 Mean & SD of Presidents' and VPs' scores in the various subscales

Country	Position	Sub-scale	Number	Mean	SD
Iran	President	MW	20	6.125	1.596
		ISV		6.725	1.129
		CHP		8.008	0.98
		EOA		7.967	1.048
		EH		7.642	0.891
	VP	MW	50	5.561	1.558
		ISV		4.147	0.942
		CHP		3.949	1.110
		EOA		5.484	1.359
		EH		6.439	1.351
France	President	MW	10	7.517	1.391
		ISV		7.683	1.076
		CHP		6.483	1.313
		EOA		8.417	0.995
		EH		8.067	0.836
	VP	MW	97	7.00	1.696
		ISV		7.182	1.730
		CHP		5.948	1.608
		EOA		7.265	1.569
		EH		6.969	1.777

Note: Model the Way (MW); Inspired a Shared Vision (ISV); Challenge the Process (CHP); Enable Others to Act (EOA); Encourage the Heart (EH).

Fig. 3.1 Comparison of French university Presidents' and Vice Presidents' opinions

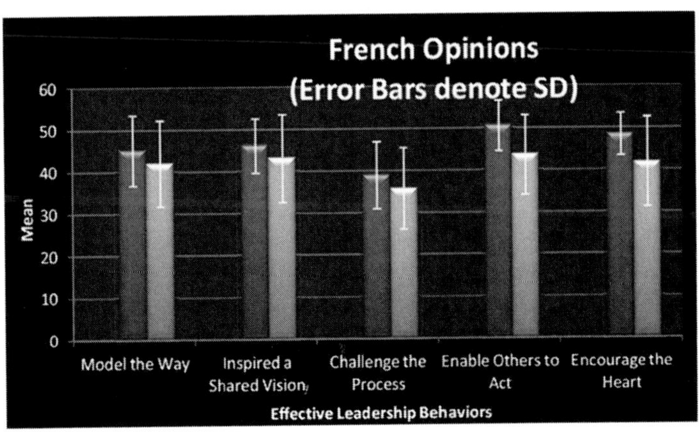

Fig.3.2 Comparison of Iranian university Presidents' and Vice Presidents' opinions

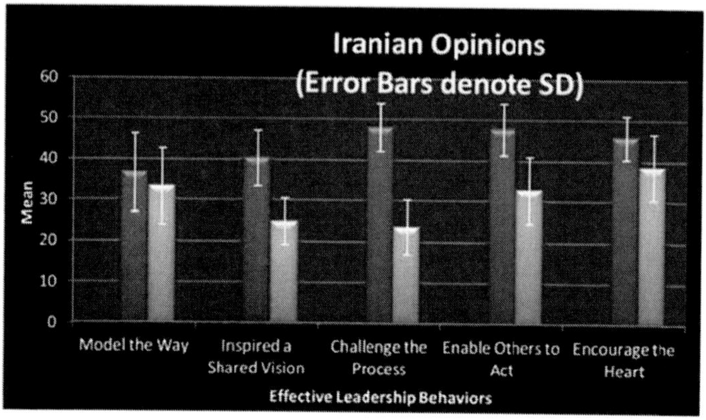

The results show that in subscales 'model the way', 'inspire a shared vision', 'encourage the heart' and 'enable others to act', French Presidents gave themselves a higher score than their Iranian counterparts. However, in subscale 'challenge the process', the Iranian Presidents gave themselves a higher score than French Presidents (Fig. 3). Considering their viewpoint, the Vice Presidents' received a higher score in all five practices of exemplary leadership. All these differences were statistically significant (p value <0.05), except for 'encourage the heart' behaviour (Fig. 4). A summary of these results is provided in Tables 3.2 and 3.3.

Fig.3.3 Comparison of Iranian and French Presidents' opinions

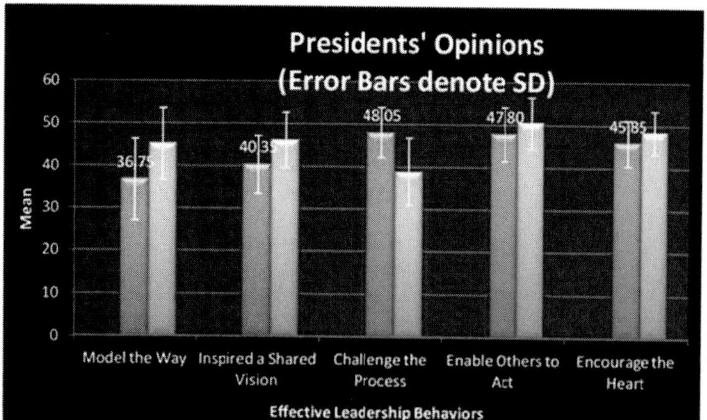

Table 3.2 Iran & France: Self-questionnaire results

Behaviour	Iran		France		p-Value
	Ave	SD	Ave	SD	
Model the way	36.75	9.57	**45.1**	8.34	**0.02**
Challenge the process	40.35	6.78	**46.1**	6.45	**0.03**
Inspire a shared vision	**48.05**	5.88	38.9	7.88	**0.006**
Enable others to act	47.08	6.29	**50.5**	5.97	0.26 (NS)
Encourage the heart	45.85	5.34	**48.4**	5.01	0.23 (NS)

Table 3.3 Iran & France: 'Others' questionnaire results

Behaviour	Iran		France		p-Value
	Ave	SD	Ave	SD	
Model the way	33.36	9.34	**42.0**	10.17	**<0.0001**
Challenge the process	24.88	5.65	**43.09**	10.38	**<0.0001**
Inspire a shared vision	23.69	6.66	**35.69**	9.65	**<0.0001**
Enable others to act	32.90	8.15	**43.59**	9.41	**<0.0001**
Encourage the heart	38.63	8.11	**41.81**	10.66	**0.04**

Fig. 3.4 Comparison of Iranian and French Vice Presidents' opinions
(Note: Left-hand columns for Iranian Presidents and right-hand columns for French Presidents.)

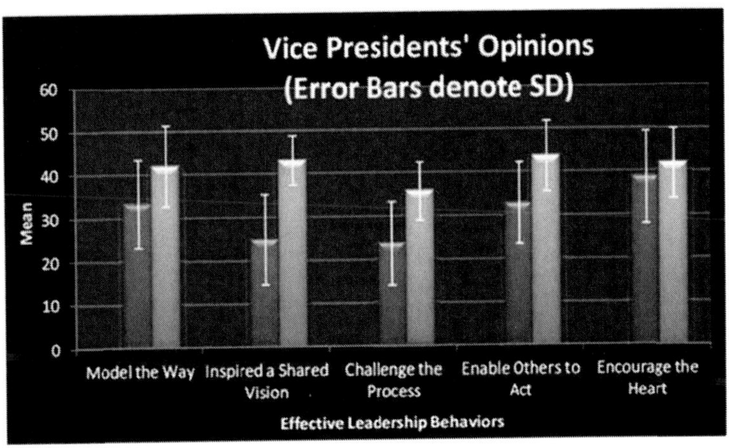

Using ANOVA, we also examined the effect of 'country' and 'respondent position' (President or Vice President) on the results for leadership behaviours. For subscale 'model the way', 'country' has a significant effect on scores ($p<0.05$), but 'position' does not ($p>0.05$). The interaction between 'country' and 'position' was not meaningful ($p>0.05$). Based on this result, we can conclude that there is a significant difference in the 'model the way' score between Iran and France. The same was true for 'inspire a shared vision' and 'encourage the heart'. For subscale 'challenge the process', the results of ANOVA showed no significant effect for the 'country' factor; i.e. there is no significant difference between the scores in Iran and France in this subscale ($p>0.05$). However, the 'position' factor had a significant effect, meaning that there is a significant difference between the Presidents' and VPs' mean scores (7.246 compared to 4.949). The interaction between 'country' and 'position' was also meaningful. For subscale 'enable others to act', both 'country' and 'position' had a significant effect on the scores. The interaction between 'country' and 'position' was also significant ($p<0.05$).

Fig.3.5 Comparison of Iranian Presidents' ('Self') and Vice Presidents' ('Manager') scores

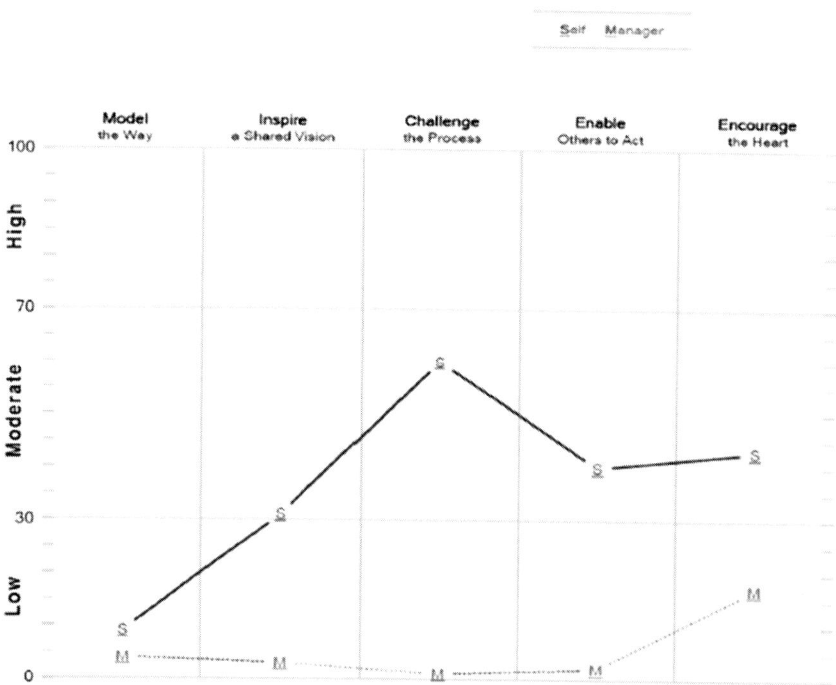

Source: Kouzes and Barry (2003–2008)

Fig.3.6 Comparison of French Presidents' ('Self') and Vice Presidents' ('Manager')

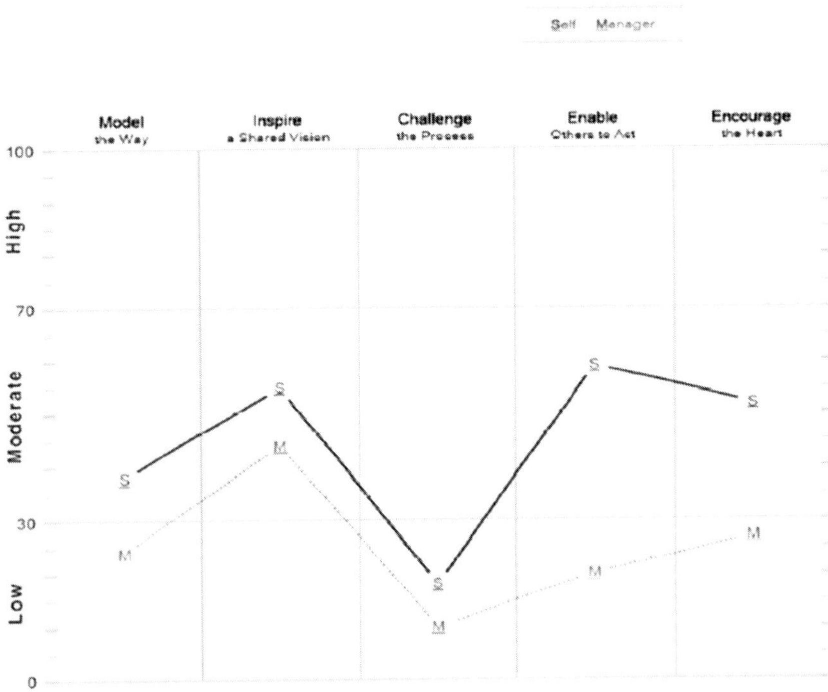

Source: Kouzes and Barry (2003–2008)

We used the services provided by Fine Points Professional Ltd. to determine the percentile of French and Iranian university Presidents' scores in the five effective leadership behaviours in comparison with the general score of all respondents to the LPI questionnaire. The results are shown in Figures 5 and 6. As is clear, university Presidents in both countries are in the low to medium percentile, especially based on the opinions of 'others' (in our case, Vice Presidents).

Open-ended questions

We also conducted content analysis on respondents' answers to our open-ended questions. We had 7 open-ended questions for Iran and 8 for France (one specific question for the LRU reform in France). Respondents to the open-ended questions in Iran were all Presidents. After reviewing the answers to each question, we classified them into a number of categories; i.e. responses that delivered a similar opinion were gathered in a group.

In response to the question 'What are the positive aspects of leadership in your institution?', the most important positive aspects in France were 'clear vision' (16 responses, 17.58% of all responses); 'listening to different points of view' and 'cooperation and team work' (13 responses; 14.28%); and 'responsibility' (12 responses, 13.18%). In Iran the most important positive aspects were 'cooperation' (6 responses, 46.15% of all responses); and 'using Islamic leadership methods', 'faith in God', 'trust', 'friendly relationship' and 'having a clear objective' (each with 2 responses, 15.38%).

In answer to the question 'What are the negative aspects of leadership in your institution?', we received 83 responses from 107 questionnaires in France, in which the main negative aspects mentioned were 'difficulty of making decision' (14 responses, 16.86%); 'lack of contact and communication' (8 responses, 9.63%) and 'lack of participation' (6 responses, 7.22%). In Iran, each respondent mentioned a different negative aspect. These included 'unavailability', 'exhaustion', 'weak social interactions with staff', 'not being completely honest with co-workers', 'incomplete power to choose my co-workers', 'inconsistency among personnel', 'low risk-taking', 'the atmosphere and environment are not suitable for growth and development' and 'some trouble-making regulations'.

In response to the third open-ended question, 'What would you recommend to improve the current leadership?', we received 84 responses in France, out of which the first item was 'strengthen communication' (13 responses, 15.48%). The next place belonged to 'having clear long-term vision and goals' (10 respondents, 11.90%). According to 7 French respondents (8.33%), the current situation 'seems good'. In Iran, 'Experts and professionals should be more involved', 'closer and stronger interaction with coworkers and staff', 'sharing responsibilities and enabling the workforce', 'trouble-making regulations should be revised' (each with 2 responses, 22.22%).

For the fourth question, 'How do managers and leading academic staff in your institution work?', the most frequent answer in France, with 17 responses (20.48%), was 'management and methods are different'. 13 (15.66%) believe that the academic staff in their university works 'in close cooperation'. 10 people (12.04%) said that 'They don't understand the question', and 5 (6.02%) responded that 'I do not know who you designate by manager'. In Iran, we received 9 responses from 20 Presidents.

The most common answer to the fifth question (with a percentage of 22.22%) revolves around two items: 'strengthen the interaction' and 'maximum participation of all faculties and staff'. For the fifth question, 94% of French respondents (79 individuals) believed that the 'new LRU Reform' was the cause of change in their institution. We will divide answers to this question into three categories: 'improvement', 'deterioration', and 'too soon to answer'.

Improvement

9 respondents believe that 'ability to set clear rules and objectives, and transparency' are definite improvements resulting from the reform (9 people, 10.71%). Secondly, respondents underline an 'increase in organized framework around projects and formalization of procedures' (5 responses, 5.65%); and according to 3 respondents, 'centralization and harmonization' are improvements brought about by the LRU reform.

Deterioration

4 people believed 'more skills are required' since LRU. Other items that seem to have deteriorated since the passing and implementation of LRU are (1 respondent each): 'financial autonomy', 'project management', 'the University has bowed to demands and orders from outside' and 'changes in staffing (down significantly)'.

In Iran, almost none of the respondents noticed – or did not wish to share – any major changes in university management in recent years. Regarding question 5, 9 out of 10 responses were simply 'No', and 1 person said that 'Because our university has only recently been founded, I cannot answer the question.'

For question 6, 'Has leadership changed in your institution in recent years?', again in Iran the majority of respondents (6 out of 9 Presidents) answered 'No'. However, 3 people believed that 'When the government changed after the Presidential Election, the leadership was handed over from one political wing to the other.' So, 'managerial stability is lacking'. In France, we received 84 responses to this question. Among these, 9 are a simple 'No' and 1 'Unfortunately no!' (10.71% in total). 10 respondents (11.90%) believed that reform had a significant impact on the leadership: 'change in Presidents is change in governance'. They believed that 'previous situation was refusal of dialogue, arbitrary decisions, and autocratic power'. On the other hand, 3 (3.57%) believed that 'Leadership depends on the personality of the leader, changing the rules is not enough to change behaviour.' 'Changes in decision making processes' were the most important improvements resulting from LRU, according to 6 of the respondents (7.14%).

For open-ended question 7, 'Have you recently witnessed conflicts because of the leadership in your institution?', we received 85 responses from France, among which 31 people (36.47%) answered 'No'. 15 respondents mentioned 'LRU' as a cause of conflicts in their institution. According to 10 of them, there are 'conflicts between the President and certain heads of department or with the General Secretariat of the university'. Among other sources of conflict in universities mentioned by the respondents are 'election process' (6 people, 7.05%); 'conflicts are not related to leadership' (3 people, 3.52%); 'power', 'failure to take into account the views of others', and 'hiring a controller, positioned in relation to policies' (each mentioned by 2 respondents, 2.35%).

Among answers to this question in Iran, we saw 4 'No's and 4 'Yes's. These conflicts according to Iranian Presidents are: 'conflict over resources', 'conflict between Presidents and administration and staff', 'conflict of personal interests', and 'lack of close interaction with faculty and staff'.

For question 8, 'Do you think the recent legal changes (LRU for example) will significantly change the leadership behaviours of university Presidents?', we received 90 responses from France. 31 respondents (34.44%) believed that 'increasing the President's power does impact his/her leadership behaviours'. However, we got different opinions as to how important this impact would be. 12 believed that LRU would 'Turn them into "business" leaders, rather than peers'. On the other hand, just one person believed that 'the President remains a peer among his peers'. Since LRU gives 'more autonomy' to the Presidents, 5 people believed that the leadership behaviour would change as a result. According to 3 respondents, LRU will 'reinforce the sense of responsibility'.

4. Discussion

The present study resulted in some interesting findings. The differences between the two countries, and the relatively low ranking of university Presidents in both countries among all respondents to the LPI questionnaire, are things that can be explained by many parameters. Discussing all possible causes of such differences is beyond the scope of just one article.

However, we discussed some of the most important aspects of our results, and explored various possible explanations for our results. We wanted to see to what extent these factors can affect the five practices of exemplary leadership that we studied in Iran and France, and focused on the context in which Iranian and French higher education leaders perform. Since almost all recent theories of leadership consider the effects of situation on leadership behaviour, we should emphasize that there are differences in the social, cultural and economic conditions, among other aspects, between Iran and France. The factors we explored were: technology, evaluation and feedback, politics (including the President's power and a centralized/decentralized system), environment and culture.

Technology

The main point to emphasize under technology is its role in communication and information, and how better communication can influence all aspects of leadership. In Iran, almost every professor (nowadays even children under 10) has a mobile phone. In almost any organization in Iran, including HE institutions, people have a culture of using traditional postal services (sending letters), using the phone or meeting face to face. Of course, if need be, they use e-mail, video conferences or other technologies. In universities, the culture of sending e-mails is most evident between students and their professors, especially for PhD students.

However, contact between administration, presidential staff and faculty is based largely on face-to-face or phone communication; the role of electronic communication is much less important than in French universities. So, having modern devices is not enough to encourage their use; having a culture of using these tools when appropriate is also needed. 'Strengthening communication' was one of the items mentioned by our respondents in both countries.

Technological advances can also be used in data collection, evaluation, communication, training, saving time and money, making people more comfortable in expressing their opinions, being more available and open to employees and to the public, increasing the clarity of functions, creating a participative environment for employees by involving them in decision-making, and finding innovative ways for rewarding and encouragement.

Evaluation and feedback

Evaluation is an important factor in improvement in any type of organization. Everybody, including the presidential team, university staff and faculty, can benefit from evaluation. The exact wording of one of the items with which the LPI examines this factor is 'Asks for feedback on how his/her actions affect other people's performance'.

In almost all organizations, evaluation helps to give people feedback on their weaknesses and strengths. This is true also for a university's structure and organization. Evaluation of universities is a fairly new concept, but one which has recently received some attention. Over the past decade, almost all European countries have imposed the evaluation of organizational and individual performance at many different levels. Quality assurance and control are surely important for the further development of the university system, and efficiency and flexibility have become dominant values. These values are the way to survive in an ever-more competitive environment, but at the same time they are also a potential threat to 'public higher education as an intellectual enterprise' (Felt and Glanz, 2005, p. 16). Evaluation helps university Presidents know to what extent they are engaged in all leadership behaviours, and lets them and others know what they have to do as a group in order to improve their leadership. One of the most important criticisms of the universities in France and Iran – based on respondents' opinions in both countries – is 'lack of evaluation and feedback processes'.

Feedback helps leaders to improve everybody's competencies; it aids transparency and clarity in leadership philosophy; it facilitates the making of appropriate adjustments according to changes in the managerial system (especially after higher education reform). Feedback also keeps more junior members of staff involved in the managerial process; allows for a better understanding of people and their needs; helps the attainment of a consensus on most decisions and the motivation of co-workers and subordinates. And, finally, feedback helps in identifying the most suitable style of leadership based on the specific situation in each individual university.

Politics

Government and politics are further key factors in both countries. Governments set general regulations and laws that may be responsible for small or big reforms in university organization. In countries like Iran that have a centralized educational system, universities are more dependent on governments than in decentralized educational systems, such as the one in France. In France there are private and other kinds of non-state institutions of higher education, particularly in Business Studies. This creates competition and limits, in a moderate way, State centralization. In Iran, even though there are private HE institutions, they are also centralized, having to abide by the government's general rules and laws. Here, university Presidents are not elected by a university council; they are appointed by the central government. Therefore, when a new national President is elected, almost all the ministers and their staff also change. So it is not just a university President's managerial or scientific qualifications that can keep him/her in his/her position.

Internal politics have an influence on all 5 practices. When somebody is elected from inside the university, he/she needs less time to establish comfortable working relationships, and people are more at ease with them. However, sometimes an elected university President may meet opposition from the loser's camp. Having an elected President has effects on 'modelling the way' behaviour. When the leader is not elected by the university staff, he/she has to try harder and to spend more time becoming familiar with his/her environment and staff in order to influence them.

Higher education can be successful in its function only if the selection and promotion of faculty, managers and students are based on their competencies. Ideology, relationships, friendships or threats should not interfere in the processes and decisions. Clear standards should be set, and everyone should work and be evaluated on that basis (Hou and Xiao, 2005). Neither Iran nor France can claim that their situation is exactly like this. In addition to competencies and scientific qualifications, personal relationships and political orientation play a significant role in the selection of university Presidents.

The existence of various interest groups within organizations can lead to internal struggles and have a direct effect on university matters. This is a question of more than party-political orientation; we are referring to the internal conflicts that arise from 'office politics'. However, this may be more evident in Iran since university Presidents are selected and appointed by central government. This means that there are more political factors influencing the appointment of a President than in France. Also in France, especially in recent years, politics have had a marked effect on university organization. According to 10 respondents, there are still, post-LRU reforms, many deficiencies in leadership. These include:

- 'Need for deep transformation of the institution';
- 'Alignment with other European countries in many areas';
- 'Difficulties in appraising';
- 'Not enough experience';
- 'Revision of conflict-resolving procedures'.

As one of the Vice Presidents believed, 'We're still stuck on establishing a consensus about the significance of governance. This may be legitimate in the present context but may not cause important changes;

however, it is essential to academic renewal. The university is not yet fully adapted to the new context established by LRU. Everything is still stalled, and the Board has not taken the measure of the role it must play.'

One of the main concerns of the LRU reform was to put an end to the paralysis in university governance by giving universities more autonomy. In France, a university President's power is complex subject, especially since the LRU law. This is especially true since the President is elected by the faculty, and therefore has closer interaction with them and with other influential bodies in the university (students, administrative staff, etc.).

In this regard, one of our respondents believed that 'a shift towards autonomy has changed many processes internally', while another agreed that there is change towards more autonomy. But it was also mentioned that 'leadership style with commitment to objectives has positive and negative aspects', and 'We have more areas to take into consideration in the shift towards greater autonomy. This requires some internal reorganization (e.g. for the management of payroll), with the human equivalent affected.'

'Autonomy' was noted both as a positive and as a negative aspect of universities. According to our respondents, we still need more time to assess the real impact of autonomy on French universities.

One of the impacts of the LRU reform according to 5.65% of respondents, which comes in second place for improvement of universities, is to have 'more formal rules and regulations and formalized management'. One Vice President mentioned: 'The university has undergone profound changes in recent years at various levels: establishment of the LRU, search for increasingly organized framework around projects, procedures for recruitment of teachers and researchers, to name only the top three. These changes were accompanied by a revision of the statutes of the university, with the emergence of new entities (the university standing committee, for example), new modes of research management, and the establishment of new committees. It is difficult to comment on … the formal rules to which they have given rise. In some cases this was an opportunity to rethink procedures; the university has bowed to demands and orders from outside.'

In Iran, and in France after LRU, politics have had a huge impact on the subject of financial resources too. Various resources are needed to maintain a good university. Material assets are not sufficient; it takes human and institutional resources too. Economic resources are important because they help supply the requisite intellectual human resources (Blau, 1973). We have seen 'lack of resources' as a negative aspect in French institutions and, in fact, as a cause for LRU reform. Moreover, 'conflict over resources' was the most common conflict mentioned by respondents in both countries; competition for access to resources causes conflict.

Environment

Globalization and the knowledge-based economic revolution have caused great transformations in the structure and function of higher education. There is increasing pressure to restructure and redesign higher education in order to meet the expectations of different stakeholders. In response to these expectations, there has been a tendency towards the decentralization, privatization and commercialization of higher education institutions. Reform strategies and criteria such as quality assurance, performance evaluation, fiscal audit, and market competition are measures that have been borrowed from the world of economics and are now generally applied to the higher education sector (Hirsch & Weber, 1999).

In reality, organizations compete with each other for resources. They are considered as input transform/output systems; i.e. they must have dynamic interaction with their environment. In these organizations, the leader's most important responsibility is to help the system to become compatible with its cnvironment and maintain a favourable balance between its inputs and outputs (Yukl, 1994).

As institutions with social relations, universities need to have dynamic contact with society as a whole and with other institutions and organizations. This type of dynamism creates specific responsibilities for leadership, since universities have to cope with the changes constantly occurring in the environment. Universities need to communicate and cooperate with the outside world. In order to fulfil the increasing expectations placed upon them, grow and strengthen their scientific relations and expand their services, universities need to have productive relations and connections with regional educational institutes, companies, hospitals, professional societies, and other scientific and industrial entities.

It is interesting to note that according to some responses to the open-ended questions in French universities, the relationship between university and outside environment was mentioned in both positive and negative terms. Two respondents mentioned 'strong involvement of the President in the development of university partnerships with many socio-economic groups' and 'the political meaning of the President (especially vis-à-vis the outside)' as positive aspects. Five people thought their universities had lack of contact with the outside world. These respondents mentioned: 'lack of contact', 'lack of communication on its business direction', 'lack of adaptability', 'lack of internal and external communication' and 'the leader works in a very isolated manner'. This was one of the main reasons for LRU reform according to one of its supporters: 'To increase contact and communication with the outside and society.'

Universities need to be responsible themselves for this increased external influence. Universities, especially large research institutions, have recently focused on generating more revenue by shifting their research projects towards inventing marketable products and technology transfer (Powers, 2003). This trend, which is called 'academic capitalism' by Slaughter and Leslie (1997), can clearly weaken the resistance of university administration and faculty to external influences on the direction of academic research. It may also distract the faculty from their primary jobs of teaching and research.

Culture

We looked closely at the results in order to try and ascertain to what extent Iranian and French Presidents are engaged in effective leadership behaviours, and to determine the impact of technology, evaluation and feedback, environment and politics on all five effective leadership behaviours. If we look at the percentile table, we see that Iranian university Presidents' scores are lower than those of their French counterparts, while French scores are not high compared to the scores of other respondents to the questionnaire in general. We can move our focus from finding reasons why these scores are low and try, instead, to identify ways to improve them. In order to do so, focusing on cultural differences may help us realize that these results and differences are to be expected. In other words, these results are acceptable considering the cultural differences.

There are some researchers who argue that at least some aspects of leadership are beyond national or geographical cultures and are universally accepted. They believe that global institutions all serve to harmonize management practices and structures (Levitt, 1983; Yavas, 1995). On the other hand, many researchers have underlined the direct impacts of culture on leadership styles. They believe that specific cultural traditions, values, ideologies and norms are 'bound to differentiate as much as or even more than structural factors between societies' (Lammers & Hickson, 1979, p. 10). Hofstede and his colleagues identified four original cultural dimensions (power distance, uncertainty avoidance, individualism–collectivism, and masculinity–femininity), and then added a fifth one: long-term and short-term orientation.

Expanding Hofstede's work, House et al (2004) in 'The GLOBE study of 62 societies' explained nine cultural dimensions: Uncertainty avoidance;

Power distance; Institutional collectivism; In-group collectivism; Gender egalitarianism; Assertiveness; Future orientation; Performance orientation; and Humane orientation.

According to the GLOBE study, Iran and France belong to different classes in each of these dimensions. For example, in 'uncertainty avoidance', the Iranian score is around 52 and the French score is around 81, almost 34% higher than the world UAI average (Unité Administrative immatriculée). Iran's score for uncertainty avoidance was the lowest of all 61 countries. Uncertainty avoidance looks at the level of tolerance for uncertainty and ambiguity within a culture. Cultures with a high uncertainty avoidance score will have a low tolerance for uncertainty and ambiguity. This means that Iranians are less concerned about ambiguity and uncertainty and are less rule-oriented. Maybe this justifies the result for 'modelling the way' behaviour – that the focus should be more on being clear and not having ambiguity in leadership philosophy and practice. Each of other cultural dimensions can influence the way leadership is perceived and practised in each country.

Nowadays, in western countries, the role of religion in politics and government is minimal. But in Iran, especially since the 1979 revolution, university Presidents have to be publicly religious, and in addition to all their other roles and responsibilities, must try to make their policies conform to Islamic values.

Explicitly or implicitly, religion is taken into consideration in both countries when someone is considered for a university presidency. In Iran, all university Presidents are Muslim, and no non-Muslim person can reach such a high position. In France, at least some scholars and academics among our respondents and interviewees do not believe that the chance to reach the position of university President is equal for members of all religions.

However, we noticed that three university Presidents had Arabic (and possibly Muslim) names in Iran. So in both countries, more or less, there are highly talented leaders who will not have the opportunity to govern a university since the factor of their religion is taken into consideration. But in this section, we want to emphasize whether Presidents can use religion to improve the five effective behaviours of leadership or not. In the open-ended response we got from Iranian Presidents, two mentioned 'using Islamic leadership' and 'faith in God' as positive aspects of their university, while none of the French respondents mentioned such things. Leaders in Iran can use religious beliefs and values in order to inspire their staff. Responsibility, doing the work in the best way they can, helping others as much as they can to make them successful, building a friendly environment, consultation, are all basic tenets in Islam – as well as being common-sense ethical rules. Since most Iranian people have at least some religious faith, Presidents can use this factor to inspire and motivate others.

Limitations of the study

We faced limitations in our study and results. These include:

1. We used Kouzes and Posner's questionnaire to evaluate effective leadership behaviours. All questionnaire-based approaches have positive and negative aspects. According to Bryman (1987), in all questionnaire-based approaches to leadership, respondents' implicit personal theories influence the individual descriptions of leaders they give when answering questions.

2. Iranian universities are governed in a centralized manner; i.e. the Presidents are appointed, not elected, and the main higher education policies are determined by central government, not by a university council. French university Presidents, however, are elected, and especially post-LRU, have great authority over various organizational issues. So we had a problem when we wanted to compare the French university system with the Iranian university structure. That is why we concluded that the only way to compare these two countries was through behaviours, while acknowledging the limitations that apply to this type of research.

3. There is a considerable lack of evidence and literature regarding university leadership. This may be due to two reasons. First, the current literature comprises mostly either descriptive or theoretical studies, and the number of field studies is small. Second, the application of 'leadership' concepts in the context of universities is fairly new.

4. University Presidents, especially in Iran, are changed frequently; the average period of presidency rarely exceeds 4 years. Therefore, it is difficult to assess their behaviours and evaluate their effectiveness in this short period of time.

5. Because of the short duration of a presidency (or vice-presidency), many respondents were reluctant to respond to the effective leadership questionnaire, since they believed they were not familiar enough with the President's behaviours.

6. Lack of cooperation on the part of Presidents and Vice Presidents in responding to and returning the questionnaire. This was predictable, and was due mainly to:

a. Their busy schedules, lack of time.

b. Some Vice Presidents were reluctant to answer as they believed it involved some kind of evaluation of the President's performance.

c. Some university Presidents in Iran believed that the questionnaire contained questions with possible political implications. However, we explained to them that a similar study was carried out in Iran about four years prior to our research.

7. Using a questionnaire as the main data-gathering tool and limiting interviews to a few respondents is one of the major limitations of this study. Due to lack of time and resources, it was not possible to interview all respondents, to gather secondary data, and evaluate the history of success and failure in each university. In order to solve this issue – at least to some extent – we used a number of open-ended questions in our questionnaire.

8. It was not feasible to study all those who are in contact with university Presidents, including students, faculty members and other university employees.

References

Allen M. (1988), 'The Goals of universities'. (The Society for Research into Higher Education, Open University Press.

Bennis W. and Nanus B., (1985). Leaders: The strategies for taking charge. New York: Harper & Row.

Besson D. and Haddaj S. (2005). L'Adaptation international des échelles de mesure: une application à la mesure de l'environnement de l'entreprise. Management International, 9(2): 1–20

Blau PM (1973). The organization of academic work. John Wiley & Sons. New York.

Felt U. and Glanz M., (2005). University autonomy in Europe: Changing paradigms in higher education policy, Special Case Studies: Decision-Making Structures and Human Resources Management in Finland, France, Greece, Hungary, Italy, the Netherlands, Spain and the United Kingdom. University of Vienna.

Hofstede G (2001). Culture's consequences: International differences in work-related values (2nd ed). Beverly Hills, CA: Sage.

House RJ. (2004). Culture, Leadership, and Organizations: The GLOBE Study of 62 Societies. Sage Publications

Kouzes JM. and Posner BZ., (2003). Leadership Challenge. 3rd Edition. John Wiley & sons, USA

McDade SA. (1988). Higher education leadership: Enhancing skills through professional development programs (Ashe Eric Higher Education Reports). Study of Higher Education

Paytas J., Gradeck R. and Andrews L., (2004). Universities and the development of industry clusters. Carnegie Mellon University, Center for Economic Development.

Powers JB. (2003). Commercializing academic research: Resource effects on performance of university technology transfer. The Journal of Higher Education, 74(1): 26–50.

Slaughter S, Leslie LL (1997). Academic capitalism- Politics, policies, and the entrepreneurial university. Baltimore: The Johns-Hopkins University Press.

Stogdill RM., (1974). Handbook of leadership: A survey of the literature. Free Press, New York, USA.

Yukl GA. (1994). Leadership in organizations. Third Edition, USA

Zaleznik A., (1977). Managers and leaders: Are they different? Harvard Business Review, May-June: 67–78.

CRM FAILURE TO APPLY OPTIMAL MANAGEMENT INFORMATION SYSTEMS: THE CASE OF THE LEBANESE FINANCIAL SECTOR

CHARBEL SALLOUM AND JASSEM AJAKA

Abstract

Financial markets in Lebanon are constrained by government influence, Islamic financial principles, and some barriers to foreign participation. Productivity in the Lebanese financial sector ranks below its occidental counterpart in spitc of the fact that regulatory, supervisory and accounting standards are generally consistent with international norms. This paper aims to give the reasons for the failure to apply an optimal management information system in the Lebanese financial sector, and to make recommendations. Our results show that the reasons include, among others, the systems themselves and their functionalities, but also companies' strategies and human capital issues.

Keywords: Financial Sector, Banks, CRM, Capital Markets.

Introduction

Customer Relationship Management (CRM) is a customer-oriented business philosophy. It involves the analysis, planning and monitoring of customer relationships using the latest information and communication technologies. Implementing a CRM project could cost up to several million dollars and requires investment in technologies and human capital. Today, the concept of CRM is synonymous with competition between companies. The challenge is not limited to gaining new customers, but also involves keeping these customers loyal to the company. Several companies have failed in implementing CRM systems. The losses were not limited to the investment; the companies also failed to gain new customers. This is why we notice some reluctance to invest in CRM. This failure constitutes the main subject for several authors who discussed the perils and pitfalls in the implementation process and/or operative performance. Nevertheless, success in implementing CRM within a company is not synonymous with economic success. In fact, evidence of the impact of CRM on business performance is scarce. The aim of this paper is to point out the reasons for failure in applying optimal management systems in the Lebanese financial sector.

1. Literature Review

Any project has an objective and a cost. Many CRM projects involving huge investments in technology fail to deliver the expected services in relation to the real cost. But how can we measure the expected results?

Grabner-Kraeuter and Moedritscher explain that the measurement of the expected results is influenced by the lack of a holistic framework for defining success criteria and metrics at the start of a CRM project. Another factor is the frequently inadequate implementation of processes for conducting ongoing performance measurement. Furthermore, a study conducted by IBM in 2004 pointed out that over 75% of companies fail to use CRM fully after it has been implemented. Finding the right system begins by defining the strategy of the company. This is why the people who have to lead a CRM project need a deep vision of the company strategy and require the resources to implement the project in full. But in most cases, organizations underestimate the level of engagement required of employees as well as of the management. The Executive management has always been focused on setting clear objectives and goals for the organization, but the Executive management's role is also essential in the final decision-making process to ensure that the team is on the right path for the organization. In the financial industry, there are several points to focus on:

- Identification of the organization's structure;
- How many systems will be integrated into the CRM system?
- How difficult is it to import the data from the core processing systems?
- Will it cost extra to program the information necessary for the organization to reach its goals?
- Which systems take priority?
- Who will be responsible for getting the file layouts or data maps to the CRM provider, and then maintaining them once the system is implemented?
- How to merge several databases into one.

The CRM system is used to give a 360-degree view of the customer. It therefore helps marketing and sales, increasing a company's market share and retaining customers. Skea found that most companies lose up to 10% of their customers per year. The main reason is dissatisfaction. Skea recommends establishing a solid historical view of the customer from all angles. In fact, this practice allows marketing directors to review trends and identify patterns in clients' behaviour. The marketing department will then be able to predict appropriate marketing actions and suggest products or services to the sales team, which can use the CRM system to track customers in real-time, regardless of the marketing channel.

DeFelice and Britt found that their CRM system allowed the lending division to double its production in one year while staff increased by only 20%. The operations department can use the system in the financial sector to respond more efficiently and quickly to the sales team's requests. Use of the system requires employees to be motivated to get more involved, and the system allows them, in return, to increase sales and then their pay. An organization should also consider identifying CRM key users throughout the organization in order to identify the areas of improvement and to put forward recommended solutions.

According to Harland, 'profit is the lifeblood of the organization; therefore its accuracy is critical.' Creating profit for the organization will take considerable effort on the management's part. Analysing a company's profits is an important marketing and executive function because it highlights where the organization's attention should be focused. Coffey and Palm found that one of the most useful reports is the profit decile report: 'The reason this is so important is that it can show (1) Who the most profitable (and least profitable) customers are; and (2) Why they are profitable or unprofitable.' They also found that the top 1% of the bank's customers can provide up to 45% of the bank's profits, and the top 20% can provide the equivalent of 17.5% of the profits. This is an astounding statistic, yet many financial institutions do not have programmes in place to retain these profitable customers. This argument is excellent to show why profit is critical to successful CRM implementation in the financial sector.

2. Empirical Study

Methodology

From the literature review, we extracted several factors that could contribute to failure in applying a CRM system. We grouped these factors into three categories:

- Institution Specificities: country, owners, local implication in Lebanon, legal status, size of the company, strategic factors encouraging investment in Lebanon, clients' origins, types of clients.
- System Specificities: existence of a CRM system, type of CRM (Transactional, Operational, Decision-Making), frequency of updates, source (internal, external);
- Use of the CRM system: cross-selling, ad-hoc relationship, reactivity, knowledge of customer, integration of several communication channels, work process, human constraints, presence of multi-players, presence of multi-sources, employees' skills and experience, legal regulations, complexity of the products.

A questionnaire was submitted to 110 banks and financial institutions in Lebanon. 32 questionnaires were selected for the completeness of the responses provided. The data were then introduced in SPSS for analysis.

3. Results

The principal objective of the analysis was to identify the main components influencing the success/failure of implementing a CRM system in the Lebanese financial sector. We checked the reliability of the scales by means of Cronbach's alpha coefficient. The reliability index for the scales used was around 0.722 for the scale of satisfaction. The preliminary factorial analysis with varimax rotation of the attributes determining the satisfaction level allows us to extract the first 6 factors that have eigenvalues higher than that for the whole (see Table 1). The total explained variance was 62.46%, thus exceeding the recommended value in social sciences. The correlations between factors of the different items expressed by means of the factorial loads are significant.

Figure 1 shows the weight of the different derived factors. As we can see, the first 6 factors explain more than 60% of the total variance, which is considered sufficient for us to limit our study to it. Table 2 shows the exploratory factorial analysis of applying the CRM in the Lebanese financial sector. Numbers represent the correlation between each component and each variable. For example, the support of dashboards by the CRM system appears to be strongly correlated to the first component.

Fig.4.1 Preliminary Factorial Analysis

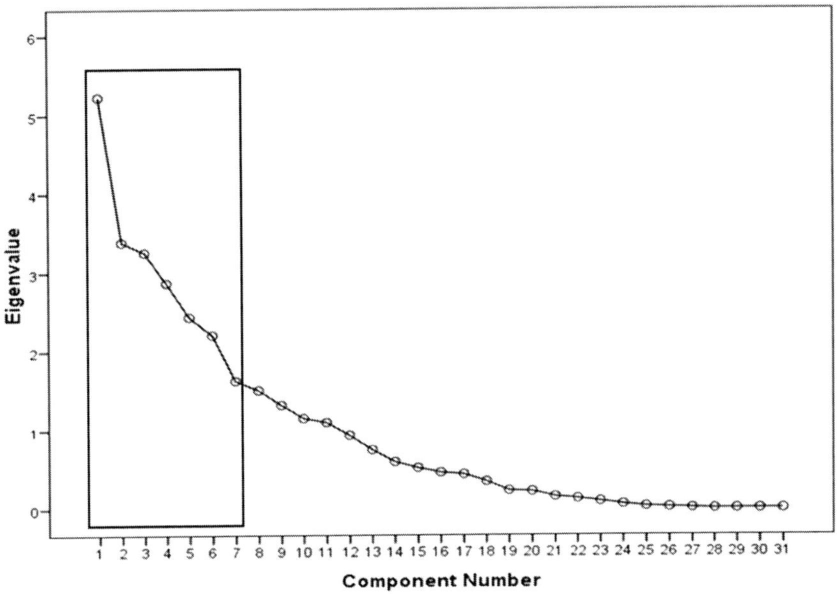

Table 4.1 Preliminary Factorial Analysis

Total Variance Explained						
Com-ponent	**Initial Eigenvalues**			**Extraction Sums of Squared Loadings**		
	Total	% of Variance	Cumula-tive%	Total	% of Variance	Cumula-tive%
1	5.225	16.854	16.854	5.225	16.854	16.854
2	3.384	10.917	27.771	3.384	10.917	27.771
3	3.254	10.496	38.267	3.254	10.496	38.267
4	2.866	9.244	47.510	2.866	9.244	47.510
5	2.432	7.844	55.355	2.432	7.844	55.355
6	2.203	7.106	62.460	2.203	7.106	62.460

Table 4.2. Exploratory Factorial Analysis of Applying the CRM in the Financial Sector

Variables	F1	F2	F3	F4	F5	F6
CRM support for dashboards	0.803	-0.357	-0.291	0.172	-0.097	0.095
CRM support for data mining	0.780	-0.219	-0.401	0.134	-0.098	0.046
Decision-making CRM	0.755	-0.071	-0.463	-0.103	-0.116	-0.195
CRM for support extraction	0.604	0.531	0.292	-0.128	0.105	0.304
CRM for support campaign management	0.500	-0.207	0.452	-0.352	0.001	-0.111
CRM update frequency	0.480	-0.317	0.329	0.245	0.343	0.282
Operational CRM	0.414	0.530	-0.053	0.277	0.525	0.068
CRM support for commercial actions	0.414	0.530	-0.053	0.277	0.525	0.068
CRM support for events management	0.403	-0.165	0.761	0.065	-0.315	-0.070
Percentage of local investors' property	0.263	0.147	0.298	-0.236	-0.362	0.219
Employees well prepared to use potential of CRM	0.256	-0.050	0.829	-0.064	-0.148	-0.051
Main category of clients	0.197	0.356	0.001	0.385	-0.411	0.050
By using the CRMs improve the knowledge of your customer	0.158	-0.480	0.074	-0.186	0.335	-0.539
CRM supports interactive channels	0.096	-0.092	0.041	0.140	-0.371	-0.118
Do you think that it is important to have quantitative skills to use CRM?	0.007	0.188	-0.303	0.201	0.395	-0.547
Number of customers	-0.052	0.233	0.074	0.363	-0.491	-0.100
Main origin of clients	-0.067	0.124	-0.084	-0.680	0.077	0.247
Foreign Investors' Property	-0.080	-0.631	-0.053	-0.070	0.212	-0.159

Do you think that the complexity of the products that you handle is an obstacle for the development of the CRM?	-0.084	0.404	0.075	-0.490	-0.172	-0.033
Do you think that the applied legal regulations are an advantage to the development of the CRM?	-0.087	0.320	-0.231	-0.279	0.068	0.450
Strategic factors that have encouraged your company to invest locally	-0.102	0.469	-0.468	0.282	-0.305	-0.086
Do you think that the presence of multi-players constitutes a difficulty for applying the CRM?	-0.149	-0.343	0.067	0.400	0.142	0.667
Number of Suppliers	-0.275	0.135	0.151	0.228	0.240	0.066
Local implication in Lebanon	-0.294	-0.148	0.387	0.251	0.370	-0.253
Number of Employees	-0.380	-0.072	0.278	0.729	-0.134	-0.132
Lebanese expatriate investors' property	-0.392	-0.393	-0.443	0.119	-0.076	0.201
Average sales per customer and per month (USD)	-0.393	-0.164	-0.153	-0.501	0.079	-0.028
Do you think that it is important to have computer skills to use the CRM?	-0.401	0.355	0.127	0.139	-0.078	-0.262
Do you think that the CRM contributes to the definition of the work process?	-0.413	-0.217	0.157	0.151	0.274	0.558

Do you think that human constraints constitute a difficulty for applying the CRM ?	-0.435	-0.406	-0.204	0.078	-0.371	0.172
CRM updated internally/ externally	-0.803	0.357	0.291	-0.172	0.097	-0.095

Fig. 4.2 Scatter plot matrix of the component scores

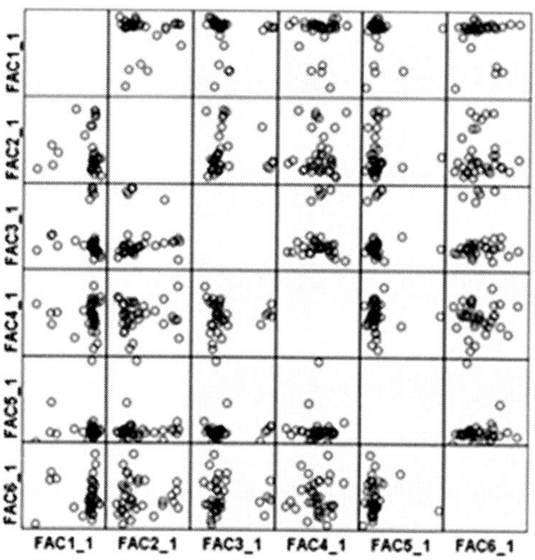

Figure 2 shows the scatter plot matrix for the different components considered. We notice that components have skewed distributions, which is because the distributions of the initial variables are skewed.

4. Discussion of the Results

Our results show that the failure of applying optimal management information systems comes from 2 main factors:

- the information system
- factors internal to the company.

The System

Our analysis shows that the system functionalities play an essential role in the success of applying optimal management system information. The results obtained mention the business functionalities (Operational CRM, Transactional CRM…) as well as the technical functionalities (opening to other sources).

Internal Factors

The strategy of a company seems to be the first factor to influence the success of applying an optimal management system. Most companies (banks, financial institutions, brokers) fail to match their use of the system with their own strategy.

Another factor playing an essential role is the skills of the employees. Although most of the companies considered that their employees were well prepared, our investigations showed that 70% of the employees questioned were unable to list the benefits of such a system.

Conclusion

In Lebanon, where the financial sector is a success story, things seem to take time to evolve. At a time when occidental financial companies are using CRM extensively to gain more customers and to enhance customer loyalty, Lebanese financial companies retain the old methods, which is confirmed by the fact that 4% of Lebanese customers account for more than 80% of all sales.

Our recommendations to the financial sector are to move forward by using CRM systems which have an open architecture. Doing so, banks, financial institutions and financial brokers will be able to compete with other regional financial sectors. At a time when secrecy is prevalent in certain countries such as Switzerland, Lebanon, Singapore and Luxembourg, Lebanon appears to be getting back its reputation as the Switzerland of the Orient. This will encourage foreign investors to invest in Lebanon. The Lebanese financial sector should be ready to offer the same service level as its occidental counterparts.

Acknowledgements

The authors would like to thanks the Lebanese Council for Scientific Research (CNRSL) for funding this research, and the Centre Supérieur de la Recherche of the USEK University for its support.

References

Coffey, J., & Palm, G. (2006). The Profit Decile Report An Eye-Opener. Bank Marketing, 38(1), 44-44. Retrieved Monday, March 27, 2006 from the Business Source Premier database.

Defelice, A., & Britt, P. (2005). Banking on Big Green. CRM Magazine, 9(11), 34-37. Retrieved Monday, March 27, 2006 from the Business Source Premier database.

Feig, N. (2005). Six Steps for Success When Buying CRM Software. Community Banker, 14(7), 38-42. Retrieved Monday, March 27, 2006 from the Business Source Premier database.

—. (2005). Six Steps for Success When Buying CRM Software. Community Banker, 14(7).

Grabner-Kraeuter, Sonja and Gernot Moedritscher. 2002. 'Alternative Approaches Toward; Measuring CRM Performance'. Paper presented at the Sixth Research Conference on Relationship Marketing and Customer Relationship Management, Atlanta, USA, 2002

Hair, J.F., Jr., Anderson, R.E., and Tatham, R.L. Multivariate Data Analysis with Readings, (2nd ed.), Macmillan Publishing Company, New York, 1987.

Harland. Profit Analysis. Retrieved April 6, 2006, from http://www.harlandfinancialsolutions.com/search/search.asp

Skea, M. (2005). Link CRM Systems to Business Processes. American Banker, pp. 10, Retrieved Monday, March 27, 2006 from the Business Source Premier database.

Appendix

Holy Spirit University of Kaslik - SURVEY

Information form to be filled out by the interviewer

Name and surname of the interviewer	
Date of the interview	
Name of the company where the interview is conducted	
Branch of industry	
Address	
Contact persons	
Particularities:	
• Number of meetings	
• Other	
Remarks	

Financial Institution Specificities

1. What is the country origin of your holding company? _______

Specify the distribution of your company's property rights:

Local investors _______%
Foreign investors _______ %
Expatriate Lebanese investors _______ %

2. What was the introduction mode in Lebanon?

Franchise ☐
Joint-venture ☐
New business ☐
Acquisition ☐
Other (Specify) ________________________

3. What is the legal structure of your company?

SNC ☐
SCS ☐
SARL ☐
SAL ☐
SCA ☐
Other (Specify) ____________________

4. What strategic factors have encouraged your company to invest locally?

The profitability of the local market ☐
The market needs (no existing banks, niche…) ☐
Geographic expansion ☐
To face the competitors ☐
Other (specify):

5. What is the main origin of your clients?

Local	☐	Europe	☐	America	☐
Asia	☐	Arab countries	☐	Africa	☐
Other	☐				

6. What is the main category of your clients?

Business ☐
Individuals ☐

7. What is the average number of your:

Employees ☐ ____
Suppliers ☐ ____
Customers ☐ ____
Sales per Customer ☐ ____

GENERALITIES RELATING TO THE CRM

8. Do you have a CRM System?

Yes ☐ No ☐

9. Does the CRM system support a Transactional CRM:

Yes ☐ No ☐ If yes, does it support:

Interactive Channels (Internet, Wap…) ☐
Customer Services (Call Centre, ASS…) ☐
Face to Face (Task Forces, CR…) ☐

10. Does the CRM system support an Operational CRM:

Yes ☐ No ☐ If yes, does it support:

Commercial Actions ☐
Campaign Management ☐
Extraction ☐
Events Management ☐

11. Does the CRM system support a Decision-making CRM:

Yes ☐ No ☐ If yes, does it contain:

Data mining ☐
Dashboard ☐

12. The CRM system is updated via:

Internal databases (production) ☐
External databases (external sources) ☐

13. The CRM system is updated:

In real time ☐
Daily ☐
Weekly ☐
Monthly ☐
As needed ☐

Using the CRM: Analysis

14. By using the CRMs do you capitalize take advantage of the wider range of products on offer (cross-selling)?

Yes ☐ No ☐

15. By using the CRMS, do you improve customer satisfaction by customizing the customer relationship (ad-hoc relationship)?

Yes ☐ No ☐

16. By using the CRMS, do you improve your reactivity?

Yes ☐ No ☐

17. By using the CRMS, do you improve your knowledge of your customer?

Yes ☐ No ☐

If yes, how? ____

____

____

18. For the B2B side, do you think that the integration of several communication channels is a plus?

Yes ☐ No ☐

If yes, how? ____

____

____

19. Do you think that the CRM contributes in defining the work process?

Yes ☐ No ☐

20. Do you think that human constraints constitute a difficulty in applying the CRM?

    Yes ☐ No ☐

21. Do you think that the presence of multi-players constitutes a difficulty for applying the CRM?

    Yes ☐ No ☐

22. Do you think that the presence of multi-sources constitutes a difficulty for applying the CRM?

    Yes ☐ No ☐

23. Do you think that the presence of multi-channels constitutes a difficulty for applying the CRM?

    Yes ☐ No ☐

24. Do you think that the CRM helps in transmitting information to better serve the customer?

    Yes ☐ No ☐

25. Do you think that your employees are well prepared to use the potential of the CRM?

    Yes ☐ No ☐

26. Do you think that it is important to have quantitative skills to use the CRM?

    Yes ☐ No ☐

27. Do you think that it is important to have computer skills to use the CRM?

    Yes ☐ No ☐

28. Do you think that it is important to have a good CRM system to better serve the customer?

    Yes ☐ No ☐

29. Do you think that the legal regulations are an advantage to the development of the CRM?

    Yes ☐ No ☐

30. Do you think that the complexity of the products that you handle is an obstacle for the development of the CRM?

    Yes ☐ No ☐

31. In comparison with your expectations, are you satisfied with the results of your CRM?

    Very satisfied ☐
    Satisfied ☐
    Poorly satisfied ☐
    Not satisfied ☐

32. In your opinion, which 3 factors influence good use of the CRM most?

____

____

____

Handling the survey

The survey was submitted to a sample of financial institutions according to the following elements:

- Elements taken into account for the survey: Banks, Financial Institution, Brokerage Institutions, and Leasing Companies in Lebanon.
- Date of the Survey.
- Handling mode: face-to-face in companies and eventually by phone.

Sample:

- 110 financial institutions and banks located in Lebanon
- People interviewed were: heads of business development departments, heads of Management Information Systems (MIS), CEOs, and Sales Managers.

The companies were:

List of official Banks

1. (01) Fransabank S.A.L.
2. (10) Banque Libano-Française S.A.L.
3. (11) B.L.C. Bank S.A.L.
4. (12) Near East Commercial Bank S.A.L.
5. (14) BLOM Bank S.A.L.
6. (16) Federal Bank of Lebanon S.A.L.
7. (22) Bank Med S.A.L.
8. (27) Audi Saradar Private Bank S.A.L.
9. (28) BBAC S.A.L.
10. (30) Banque Lati S.A.L.
11. (35) Banque Pharaon et Chiha S.A.L.
12. (36) Banque de crédit national S.A.L.
13. (39) Byblos Bank S.A.L.
14. (44) Lebanese Canadian Bank S.A.L.
15. (48) Banque de l'industrie et du travail S.A.L.
16. (52) Intercontinental Bank of Lebanon S.A.L.
17. (56) Bank Audi S.A.L. – Audi Saradar Group
18. (58) Bank of Kuwait & the Arab World S.A.L.
19. (63) Lebanese Swiss Bank S.A.L.
20. (68) Société Nouvelle de la Banque de Syrie et du Liban S.A.L.
21. (71) Allied Bank S.A.L.
22. (75) Bank of Beirut S.A.L.
23. (80) Jammal Trust Bank S.A.L.
24. (92) Banque de la Bekaa S.A.L.
25. (93) BEMO - Banque européenne pour le Moyen-Orient S.A.L.
26. (94) Lebanon and Gulf Bank S.A.L.
27. (95) Saudi Lebanese Bank S.A.L.
28. (101) Al-Mawarid Bank S.A.L.
29. (103) CreditBank S.A.L.
30. (104) United Credit Bank S.A.L.
31. (105) Bank al-Madina S.A.L.
32. (108) First National Bank S.A.L.
33. (110) M.E.A.B. S.A.L.
34. (3) Banque Misr Liban S.A.L.
35. (34) Syrian Lebanese Commercial Bank S.A.L.
36. (53) Crédit Libanais S.A.L.
37. (62) North Africa Commercial BankS.A.L.
38. (73) National Bank of Kuwait (Lebanon) S.A.L.

39. (84) Al-Ahli International Bank S.A.L.
40. (109) Al-Baraka Bank Lebanon (B.B.L.) S.A.L.
41. (124) Arab Finance House S.A.L. (Islamic Bank)
42. (126) Lebanese Islamic Bank S.A.L.
43. (19) Société Générale de Banque au Liban (SGBL) S.A.L.
44. (98) Standard Chartered Bank S.A.L.
45. (5) Arab Bank plc.
46. (9) Rafidain Bank
47. (17) The Saudi National Commercial Bank
48. (90) Arab African International Bank
49. (2) Banca di Roma S.P.A.
50. (6) Banque Nationale de Paris Intercontinentale
51. (7) HSBC Bank Middle East Ltd.
52. (67) Bank Saderat Iran
53. (85) Habib Bank Limited
54. (115) CitiBank N.A.
55. (33) Audi Saradar Investment Bank S.A.L.
56. (41) Banque de l'Habitat S.A.L.
57. (43) Finance Bank S.A.L.
58. (111) BlomInvest S.A.L.
59. (113) Mediterranée Investment Bank S.A.L.
60. (114) Crédit Libanais Investment Bank S.A.L. (1)
61. (118) Arab Investment Bank S.A.L. (1)
62. (121) Fransa Invest Bank S.A.L.
63. (123) Byblos Invest Bank S.A.L.
64. (125) Arab Finance Investment House S.A.L. (Islamic Bank) (1)

List of official financial brokerage companies

65. (1) Merril Lynch, Pierce, Fenner and Smith (Middle East) S.A.L.
66. (2) S.C.S. Beyrouth S.A.L.
67. (3) World Investment Services S.A.L.
68. (4) 'Investa' Financial Planning Services S.A.L.
69. (5) Arab International Development and Investment Company S.A.L.
70. (6) SNA Asset Management (SNAM) S.A.L
71. (8) Beirut Brokerage Corporation S.A.L.
72. (9) Optimum Invest S.A.L.
73. (10) Melkart Capital S.A.L. (1)

List of official leasing companies

74. (1) Société CrediLease S.A.L.
75. (2) Société Libanaise de Leasing S.A.L. 'Leasing'
76. (3) Arab Leasing S.A.L.

List of official financial institutions

77. (1) Arab Finance Corporation S.A.L.
78. (2) Investment Trading Company S.A.L.
79. (5) Crédit Commercial et Foncier S.A.L.
80. (6) SOGELEASE Liban S.A.L.
81. (7) Société d'investissements financiers S.A.L.
82. (8) Société financière du Liban S.A.L.
83. (9) BEMO sécurisation S.A.L.
84. (10) FIDUS S.A.L.
85. (11) Capital Investment Services S.A.L.
86. (12) Lebanon Invest S.A.L.
87. (13) Gulf Finance & Investment Company S.A.L.
88. (14) Libano-Française Finance S.A.L.
89. (16) G. T. Asseily & Co. S.A.L.
90. (17) Saradar Investment House S.A.L.
91. (18) Financial Funds Advisors International S.A.L.
92. (19) Middle East Capital Group (MECG) S.A.L.
93. (22) Allied Business Investment Corporation S.A.L. (Abicorp)
94. (23) BLC Finance S.A.L.
95. (24) Halawi Investment Trust S.A.L.
96. (25) Finance Center Corporation (FCC) S.A.L.
97. (26) Crédit Financier S.A.L.
98. (27) Kafalat S.A.L.
99. (28) Capital finance Company S.A.L.
100. (29) Société Libanaise de Factoring - Solifac S.A.L.
101. (30) Crédit Financier S.A.L.
102. (31) Al Mawarid Financial Services S.A.L.
103. (32) Credit Trust S.A.L.
104. (34) MENA Capital S.A.L.
105. (35) HSBC Financial Services (Lebanon) S.A.L.
106. (36) Capital Investment Corporation S.A.L. (1)
107. (37) BOB Finance S.A.L. (2)
108. (38) Amwal Invest S.A.L. (3)
109. (39) Amex (Middle East) B.S.C. (4)
110. (40) Crédit Financier Invest S.A.L. (5)

LA RELOCALISATION DANS LE PAYS D'ORIGINE EST-ELLE UN ACTE DE RSE, CREATRICE D'EMPLOIS ?

CATHERINE MERCIER-SUISSA

Résumé

De nombreuses PME délocalisent leurs activités dans des pays à bas coûts. Ces pratiques sont souvent décriées en raison des conditions de production dans les pays d'accueil et des conséquences sur l'emploi dans les pays d'origine. Les PME s'exposent à un risque de réputation. Les pouvoirs publics proposent des aides favorisant le développement des activités productives en France. Face à ces critiques et ces incitations, on observe la relocalisation des activités de certaines PME, qui est présentée comme un acte de RSE. Mais l'étude de quatre cas d'entreprises en Rhône-Alpes semble indiquer que la relocalisation d'activités ne génère pas de nombreuses créations d'emploi. Dès lors, les mesures prises par les pouvoirs publics en faveur des relocalisations au regard de pratiques de RSE, créatrices d'emploi, sont discutées.

Mots clé : RSE, PME, délocalisation, relocalisation, emplois

Introduction

Les délocalisations sont au cœur des préoccupations actuelles des décideurs politiques et des praticiens du développement économique. Pourtant, elles font débat dans la sphère économique, car les conséquences de la délocalisation en termes de pertes d'emplois dans le pays d'origine interrogent l'observateur. Les délocalisations vers les pays à bas coûts soulèvent un problème relatif à la RSE dans son pays d'origine. En délocalisant dans des pays à bas coûts, des emplois sont détruits dans le pays d'origine qui ne sont pas compensés par les emplois indirects (dans le transport, les services commerciaux et financiers) créés. Les salariés licenciés ne sont pas réembauchés dans ces emplois souvent plus qualifiés. D'où les critiques virulentes des salariés concernés et des collectivités locales frappées par des vagues de licenciement. En outre, des pays d'accueil se livrent à du dumping social et le revendiquent même, pour attirer les activités délocalisées (Mercier-Suissa, 2011). Ces pratiques mettent en péril les acquis et modèles sociaux et l'entreprise peut faire l'objet de charges virulentes de la part de ses parties prenantes : syndicats, salariés, ONG, médias… Dès lors, si l'entreprise qui a délocalisé dans un pays à bas coût relocalise dans son pays d'origine, elle peut ainsi renforcer son image d'entreprise citoyenne sur son territoire. Ainsi, force est de constater qu'un certain nombre de chefs d'entreprise, ayant relocalisé, mettent en avant le fait que cette décision est un acte de de RSE.

Toutefois, des cas récents en Europe, et plus particulièrement en Italie, semblent indiquer que la relocalisation s'effectue sous certaines conditions ; fin 2011, Fiat a fait part à travers son plan « Fabbrica Italia » de son intention de relocaliser la production de la Panda de Pologne en Italie. En contrepartie de cette relocalisation, le constructeur a bénéficié d'une sortie des conventions collectives donnant lieu aux concessions suivantes : une production 24 heures sur 24 et 6 jours par semaine, le nombre d'heures supplémentaires augmenté et le temps de pause déjeuner réduit à 30 minutes. Peut-on dès lors parler de RSE en Italie ?

Face à ces constats, on peut s'interroger pour savoir si, une stratégie de relocalisation des activités productives de la PME sur son territoire d'origine est un acte de RSE ? La relocalisation d'activités s'accompagne-t-elle de nombreuses créations d'emplois dans le pays d'origine ? Pourquoi les PME relocalisent-elles leurs activités ? Pour répondre à ces questions nous allons dans une première partie, préciser les concepts liés à notre questionnement, que sont le phénomène de relocalisation, notre objet de recherche qui concerne la PME et le lien qui existe entre RSE et relocalisation. Puis dans une seconde partie, nous présenterons quatre cas d'entreprises ayant relocalisé, afin de montrer quels sont les déterminants des relocalisations et si la relocalisation est bien créatrice d'emplois en France ? Et peut-elle être assimilée à un acte de RSE ? Puis, nous discuterons, dans une troisième partie, des mesures actuellement mises en place par les pouvoirs publics français pour inciter les entreprises à relocaliser au regard des pratiques de RSE visant à créer des emplois.

1. Concepts liés à notre questionnement

La relocalisation : définitions et déterminants

Bouba-Olga (2006) définit la relocalisation comme étant le retour vers un pays développé d'activités ou d'unités de production précédemment délocalisées dans un pays à bas coûts de production. Chanteau (2001b, p.88) indique que la relocalisation est « *l'opération inverse de rapatriement « annulant » une délocalisation* ». Mouhoub El Mouhoud (2006) quant à lui indique qu'au sens strict, la relocalisation est définie comme étant :

« le retour dans le pays d'origine d'unités productives, d'assemblage ou de montage antérieurement délocalisées sous diverses formes dans les pays à faibles coûts salariaux ».

Au sens large, elle est définie comme :

« le ralentissement du processus de délocalisation vers les pays à bas salaires, c'est-à-dire la remise en cause des décisions de délocalisation ou la non-délocalisation dans les secteurs sensibles à la compétition par les coûts ».

Nous retiendrons pour nos propos de ces différentes définitions de la relocalisation, le fait qu'elles prennent en compte la notion de bas salaire ou pays à faibles coûts de production. Même si à notre sens, la relocalisation ne concerne pas uniquement des pays à bas coûts salariaux, il est à retenir que les faibles coûts salariaux, bien souvent, reflètent également l'existence de faibles coûts sociaux, de conditions de travail très dégradées et de manière plus large de dumping social. Dès lors, un déterminant de la relocalisation pourrait bien être la révélation par des ONG ou des médias, de pratiques peu éthiques de la part de PME qui ont délocalisé, ce qui impacterait la notoriété de ces entreprises, et leur ferait courir un risque de réputation (Mercier-Suissa, 2009).

Notre objet d'étude, la PME qui a relocalisé

Rappelons que notre objet d'étude est la PME. Ces entreprises sont des organisations de moins de 250 salariés travaillant à temps complet et réalisant un chiffre d'affaires annuel inférieur à 50 millions d'euros (INSEE, 2010). La faiblesse de leur taille, qui a par ailleurs, fait l'objet de nombreux travaux[1], procure un désavantage à la PME en matière de communication. En effet, dans le cas d'une campagne de dénigrement sur internet par exemple, la PME risque d'avoir moins de ressources financières disponibles pour se défendre qu'une FMN qui subirait la même chose. Dès lors, la relocalisation pourrait s'expliquer par la volonté qu'a la PME d'éviter d'être soupçonnée de pratiques peu éthiques et d'être reconnue comme socialement responsable (Mercier-Suissa et Belbenoit-Avich, 2009). Car, relocaliser dans le pays d'origine devrait avoir pour conséquence la création d'emplois dans ce pays, contribuant ainsi à améliorer la croissance économique.

C'est pourquoi nous allons chercher à savoir dans quelle mesure la relocalisation permet-elle le retour à l'emploi de salariés. Pour ce faire, il nous faut identifier les différents déterminants de la relocalisation et essayer d'apprécier les conséquences sur l'emploi. Dans un premier temps nous allons présenter ces déterminants et nous les complèterons avec l'étude empirique de quatre cas d'entreprises en seconde partie. Au travers de notre étude empirique, nous tenterons d'apprécier les effets de la relocalisation sur l'emploi.

Déterminants de la relocalisation de la PME

Dans des écrits antérieurs (Bouveret-Rivat et Mercier-Suissa 2008, et Mercier-Suissa, 2011), nous avons déjà présenté une typologie des déterminants des relocalisations à partir d'une revue de la littérature sur ce thème. Nous avons fait ressortir deux groupes de déterminants. Le premier groupe correspond aux raisons qui conduisent les entreprises à relocaliser leurs activités suite aux problèmes rencontrés dans le pays d'accueil ; le second groupe concerne les déterminants des relocalisations relatifs aux transformations de l'avantage comparatif du pays d'origine.

Ainsi dans le premier groupe, la relocalisation peut s'expliquer par la hausse des salaires locaux et la faiblesse de la productivité du travail dans le pays d'accueil (Bouba-Olga, 2006), par la suppression des subventions, la baisse de la qualité des produits fabriqués ou des services proposés, par la hausse des coûts de contrôle (copie, pertes, vols…), et par la hausse des

[1] L'effet de la taille sur la pérennité des activités de la PME, notamment à l'internat ional, fait débat. S'il est vrai qu'elle participe à la fragilisation de l'entreprise sur le s marchés, celle-ci ayant peu de poids face aux grandes structures, et limite ses cap acités de développement à l'international (Calof, 1993, 1994), la petite taille perme t à la PME d'être beaucoup plus réactive, ayant un organe décisionnel beaucoup pl us restreint. Liesch et Knight (1999) avancent même que la petite taille peut deveni r un avantage dans la conclusion de transactions internationales.

coûts de transport. Enfin, la dégradation de l'image de l'entreprise est un élément également évoqué (Gasmi et Grolleau, 2002).

Sur ce dernier point, il convient de signaler que les associations de consommateurs, les médias, les ONG et certains syndicats sont en mesure de faire peser sur les entreprises un risque économique et juridique par des campagnes de dénigrement, par le boycott des produits, par des procès, que ces dernières relocaliseraient (Mercier-Suissa et Belbenoit-Avich, 2009).

Les parties prenantes (ONG, par exemple) peuvent exercer une pression telle sur l'entreprise (Grolleau, Lakhal et Mzoughi, 2004), que celle-ci peut voir dans la satisfaction des attentes des parties prenantes, un facteur clef de succès d'une valeur au moins égale à celle de la réduction des coûts de production en étant délocalisée. C'est pourquoi, faute de pouvoir améliorer les conditions de production à l'étranger et les conséquences qui en découlent sur son image, l'entreprise relocalisera.

Dans le second groupe, les principaux déterminants explicatifs des relocalisations dans le pays d'origine concernent les avantages comparatifs du pays d'origine que l'on redécouvre ou qui se sont modifiés en faveur de l'entreprise avec le temps.

Ainsi, la créativité et le savoir-faire, le regroupement d'activités dans des clusters, la production de proximité (rapidité du réassort, flux tendus), l'automatisation, les gains de productivité, les mesures fiscales favorables (zones rurales, zones franches…), et l'attitude nationaliste de la clientèle sont autant d'éléments qui peuvent expliquer une relocalisation (Mercier-Suissa et Bouveret-Rivat, 2008).

Le lien entre RSE et la relocalisation des PME : la création d'emplois

La RSE n'est pas un nouveau concept, même si elle fait l'objet d'une forte attention actuellement. Elle s'est développée en France depuis le début du XXème siècle. Elle traite des relations entre l'entreprise et la société. Ainsi, plusieurs problématiques sont abordées dans la littérature, mais très peu concernent les manifestations de la RSE pour une PME dans le cadre d'une relocalisation.

Même si on constate aujourd'hui la mise en place d'une législation pour favoriser la RSE dans les entreprises, tant au niveau national (loi dite NRE, Nouvelles Régulations Economiques) que régional (Livre Vert en 2001 pour l'Union européenne), ou encore international (le Pacte Mondial), ceci concerne davantage les grandes entreprises que les PME. Il existe une volonté de normalisation de la RSE, par exemple, la norme ISO

14 000 relative à l'environnement, ou encore la norme ISO 26 000, dont l'objectif est de servir de cadre aux entreprises souhaitant avoir une démarche de RSE, mais il y a encore assez peu d'initiatives en faveur de la RSE, concernant la dimension sociale, dans les PME.

Toutefois, même si peu de travaux s'intéressent à la RSE dans les PME jugées en retard dans ce domaine, ces dernières s'y engagent progressivement soit en s'appuyant sur les pratiques des Grandes Entreprises, soit en appliquant un cadre fourni par un partenaire extérieur (par exemple, un donneur d'ordre, un client…) (Mercier-Suissa, 2009). La RSE pour la PME désigne des actions visant à concilier responsabilité sociale et logique économique et financière. La notion de RSE qui peut être mise en avant lorsqu'il y a relocalisation peut avoir deux origines : une **RSE subie** et une **RSE choisie**.

Par **RSE subie** nous entendons, que l'attitude responsable de la PME provient en fait de la crainte de voir son image se dégrader du fait de sa production à l'étranger. Contrairement aux grandes entreprises tel Danone, Total, Lafarge… qui mènent des actions éducatives et sanitaires en faveur de populations défavorisées, les PME, de par leur petite taille et le manque de ressources, n'ont pas les moyens financiers de mener de telles actions. En revanche, elles peuvent afficher leur bonne volonté en proposant des produits issus du commerce équitable, des produits respectueux de l'environnement et surtout des produits qui sont fabriqués dans le plus strict respect du Droit du travail. Ces deux derniers points attirent particulièrement notre attention dans la mesure où sous la pression croissante exercée par la société civile, ajoutée aux menaces de boycott (Trautmann, 2004) des produits fabriqués à l'étranger, la relocalisation en France apparait maintenant synonyme de respect des normes sociales de production pour les consommateurs (étude CEDRE/IFOP, 2011). A la question : *« Etes-vous, tout à fait d'accord, plutôt d'accord, plutôt pas d'accord ou pas du tout d'accord avec le fait qu'un produit soit fabriqué en France, implique l'assurance que le produit ait été fabriqué selon des normes sociales respectueuses des salariés ? »,* 87% des français interrogés étaient tout à fait et plutôt d'accord[2]. Comme le souligne Allemand S. (p.139) :

> « *Un des premiers principes de la RSE, consiste pour l'entreprise à tenir compte des différents acteurs économiques, sociaux et politiques concernés par son activité.* ».

---

[2] Cedre/IFOP, novembre 2011, regards croisés français et chefs d'entreprise.

Dès lors, pour un chef d'entreprise, relocaliser en France apparait bien avoir comme conséquence de faire apparaître cette action comme une pratique de RSE au regard de ces considérations sociales, même si à la base, le chef d'entreprise relocalise pour d'autres raisons (faible qualité, hausse des coûts, etc…). Dans le cas de **la RSE choisie**, l'entreprise relocaliserait afin d'assurer son rôle d'entreprise citoyenne au sens où elle paye ses impôts et crée des emplois dans son pays d'origine. Les récentes mesures en faveur des relocalisations et surtout, la communication qui est faite autour par les pouvoirs publics, mais également par les entreprises, indique que la relocalisation est un choix qui repose sur des considérations éthiques. Nombreux sont les dirigeants de PME, qui ont relocalisé et qui déclarent :

> « *Dans un environnement concurrentiel comme le nôtre, le Made in France peut être un atout pour gagner des parts de marché* » explique Philippe Peyrard, Directeur général délégué de la coopérative des opticiens ATOL, ou encore

> « *S'attacher à produire en France est un acte citoyen qui doit impliquer les politiques et motiver les entrepreneurs. C'est un challenge que nous nous sommes fixés pour nous différencier auprès de nos clients dans une démarche RSE de fond* » selon Vincent GRUAU, PDG de Majencia.[3].

La création d'emplois

Toute opération de délocalisation se traduit par une destruction d'emplois dans le pays d'origine et par la création d'emplois dans le pays d'accueil. A cela il faut rajouter des destructions d'emplois induites et de manière symétrique, des créations d'emplois indirectes. A titre d'exemple, une entreprise qui produit à l'étranger et qui réimporte ses produits va faire travailler des transporteurs, compagnies d'assurance, banques etc. … et donc la délocalisation génère des créations d'emplois indirects. Mais en même temps, quand une entreprise délocalise, ce sont des fournisseurs, des sous-traitants, voir l'emploi local (commerce, immobilier…) qui sont affectés par le départ de l'entreprise et par la moindre activité qui en résulte. En sens inverse, lors d'une relocalisation des emplois sont détruits dans le pays d'accueil mais on peut s'attendre à ce que des emplois, plus qualifiés, soient créés dans le pays d'origine. Il est excessivement difficile pour ne pas dire impossible, d'isoler le nombre d'emplois indirects détruits par une délocalisation et ceux qui sont créés par le retour des activités dans

[3] Rapport CEDRE/IFOP, 2011

le pays d'origine. Dès lors, il nous semble intéressant de nous interroger sur la nature des emplois détruits et créés par ces mouvements de localisation des activités. Sans avoir les moyens de chiffrer précisément le nombre d'emplois détruits et créés au niveau macroéconomique, nous allons essayer d'identifier le type d'emplois détruits et créés par des PME qui ont relocalisé. Pour ce faire nous avons mené des entretiens auprès de PME qui avaient relocalisé en France et qui mettaient en avant sur leur site, ou dans la presse, leurs pratiques de RSE, au regard de considérations sociales. Ainsi notre étude empirique va nous permettre à la fois d'expliquer les déterminants de la relocalisation et de voir dans quelle mesure la relocalisation a permis la création d'emplois.

2. Des cas d'entreprise pour identifier les determinants de la relocalisation et les conséquences sur l'emploi

Présentation de la méthodologie

Les études de cas présentées dans cette communication sont en majorité issues d'une étude que nous avons menée entre 2009 et juin 2011, pour la région Rhône-Alpes (projet cible 2009) dans le cadre du projet Damier[4] . Cette étude comporte deux volets principaux. Le premier volet a eu pour objectif de *« quantifier le phénomène de délocalisations-relocalisations des entreprises rhône-alpines sur la période 1990-2009 »*, afin de pouvoir identifier quelles étaient les entreprises qui avaient délocalisé puis relocalisé. Le deuxième volet a été de réaliser une étude qualitative centrée sur le phénomène de relocalisation. Nous allons donc reprendre dans notre communication quatre cas d'entreprises que nous avons étudiés qui nous apparaissent significatifs compte tenu de la diversité des secteurs et de la nature des activités qui ont été délocalisées.

Pour mener l'étude quantitative, nous avons relevé les informations fournies par l'agence d'informations professionnelles *Bref Rhône-Alpes*, qui réalise une collecte d'informations systématique des entreprises ayant un établissement en Rhône-Alpes et un chiffre d'affaires inférieur à 3 millions d'euros. Ces informations sont issues de journaux agréés d'annonces légales, de déclarations spontanées des entreprises auprès de cette agence et d'enquêtes hebdomadaires auprès de divers réseaux professionnels. A partir de ces données, utilisées dans l'étude quantitative,

[4] cf. Chanteau JP et Mercier-Suissa C. (dir.), DAMIER. Délocalisation d'Activités et Mobilité Internationale des Entreprises en Rhône-Alpes. Rapport final 4 juin 2011, projet Cible 2009, rendu à la Région Rhône-Alpes, juin 2011, 38 p.

il a été possible de constituer un échantillon d'entreprises Rhône-alpines ayant relocalisé. Ainsi, nous avons recensé 17 entreprises Rhône-alpines ayant relocalisé dans la période de 1993 à 2010. Les informations disponibles ont été complétées par des entretiens avec des experts (par exemple, Entreprise Rhône-Alpes International (ERAI)…).

La plupart des entreprises identifiées ont été contactées pour procéder à un entretien en face à face, à partir d'un guide d'entretien que nous avons élaboré. Dans le cadre de cette communication, nous avons sélectionné quatre cas de relocalisation en Rhône-Alpes qui concernent des PME (Dynastar, Mafelec, Smoby, PCI SCEMM). Compte tenu de la taille de l'échantillon, il est à noter que ce travail est exploratoire, d'autant plus qu'il concerne des phénomènes émergents, notamment celui du lien entre relocalisation et RSE. Pour chaque cas, nous allons présenter un diagnostic interne et externe, récapitulé dans un tableau, suivi d'un commentaire qui résume les conséquences sur les ressources humaines.

Présentation des cas

Le cas de Dynastar – Groupe Rossignol

La PME Dynastar, créée en 1963, est localisée en Haute-Savoie à Sallanches. Elle appartient au groupe Rossignol depuis 1967. Elle emploie environ 180 personnes. Elle a pour activité la fabrication d'articles de sport d'hiver, notamment la production de ski. A la suite du rachat de Rossignol en 2005 par Quicksilver, la nouvelle direction décide de délocaliser une partie de la production du site de Sallanches (les skis junior) en Chine. Mais rencontrant de grosses difficultés financières, et suite au rachat du groupe Rossignol par le consortium « Chartreuse et Mont Blanc » à Quicksilver en 2008, un an après, une grande partie de la production est relocalisée en France dans l'usine Dynastar de Sallanches. C'est pour ne plus subir « l'effet d'inertie » lié au délai de transport des matières premières de l'Europe vers l'Asie et des produits de l'étranger vers la France, et, constatant que le coût de production d'un ski est lié à 70% aux matériaux employés, que l'entreprise a relocalisé. En accord avec la nouvelle stratégie et fort de ces constats, la Direction décide en 2011 de renforcer la production du site de Sallanches en ramenant plusieurs lignes de production de Chine, afin de faire face notamment à des charges fixes élevées tout en maintenant 10 à 15 % des activités en sous-traitance. En résumé, ce que nous pouvons retenir de cette expérience pour la société Dynastar, et plus largement pour le groupe Rossignol, est que la relocalisation vise à :

- maintenir un site de production en France et en optimiser les charges,
- avoir une meilleure maîtrise de la gestion des stocks en produisant en flux tendu tout en suivant au plus près la courbe saisonnière des commandes,
- symboliser un savoir-faire local haut de gamme capable de répondre notamment à la « personnalisation » des demandes clients.

Pour résumer la situation, nous avons réalisé un diagnostic tant interne qu'externe (cf. tableau n°1), afin de mettre en évidence les déterminants de la relocalisation.

Tableau 5.1 Diagnostic de la relocalisation de Dynastar (groupe Rossignol)

Forces	Faiblesses
+ Retour à son cœur de métier + Produits de haut de gamme + Gestion de production en flux tendu + Adaptation des produits à la demande, voire personnalisation + Offrir plus de service aux clients + Réduction des délais	- Situation financière difficile
Opportunités	**Menaces**
+ Rachat par un consortium + Valorisation du territoire	- Importance des matériaux utilisés (70% des coûts de production) (meilleure qualité en France)

La relocalisation de l'activité de l'entreprise en France s'explique principalement par le fait que les investissements, liés à la délocalisation, ne permettaient pas de rentabiliser véritablement l'activité. C'est pourquoi l'entreprise a été de nouveau rachetée. La nouvelle direction a décidé alors de relocaliser les activités en France pour améliorer la rentabilité.

Impact sur les ressources humaines

Les plans sociaux de 2005, puis de 2009 n'ont pas favorisé un bon climat social dans le groupe et notamment chez Dynastar. Ces suppressions d'emplois, touchant majoritairement des « gens du pays », ont mobilisé l'ensemble de la vallée et la presse locale. Il faut toutefois noter que le 2ème plan de licenciement n'a touché aucune personne de la production, mais des salariés employés à la R&D, aux achats,... c'est-à-dire aux fonctions supports. C'est dans un contexte difficile que le nouveau directeur, M. Mimmo Salerno, est arrivé en juillet 2009 avec notamment pour mission de gagner à nouveau la confiance des salariés dans la perspective de préparer la relocalisation. L'enjeu consistait également à remobiliser les effectifs, toujours très attachés à leur entreprise, en leur présentant le projet de réorganisation globale du groupe et la valorisation du site de Sallanches. Cette démarche a donné lieu à une véritable campagne de communication interne. Elle s'est traduite par des actions concrètes :

- renouvellement d'une partie de l'outil de production ;
- proposition de nouveaux projets : les « 5S », c'est une technique de management japonaise visant à l'amélioration continue des tâches effectuées dans les entreprises, des campagnes d'investissements et de modernisation.

Il a fallu renouer un dialogue « vrai » avec les partenaires sociaux sur le thème « je dis ce que je fais / je fais ce que je dis ». Le projet de relocalisation est donc au centre de cette approche. Un an après l'arrivée du nouveau directeur et dans une phase économique et financière plutôt rassurante pour le groupe, le site de Sallanches déploie une véritable politique de GRH, avec pour objectif principal de rendre plus claire et lisible cette politique auprès de l'ensemble du personnel. Les différents axes entrepris sont :

- Mise en place d'un accord de modulation horaire, avec :
    - Formalisation des fiches de postes et des référentiels de compétences (logique adéquation besoins / compétences) ;
    - Reprise des entretiens individuels ;
    - Définition d'une politique de rémunération adaptée : cohérences entre les statuts, classifications et les postes ;
    - Proposition de plans de carrières afin que les salariés puissent se projeter, évaluer les marges de progression ;

D'une manière plus large les grands chantiers RH sont les suivants :

- Un projet d'accord GPEC ;
- Un plan senior ;
- Un plan de réduction de la pénibilité au travail ;
- Le développement des compétences sur les nouvelles technologies (plan de formations).

Bien que la fonction RH soit pilotée depuis le siège de Rossignol à St Jean de Moirans, en fonction des stratégies du groupe, le site Dynastar de Sallanches emploie une Responsable RH et son assistante. Ainsi dans ce cas présent, on peut considérer que la relocalisation a eu pour conséquence d'améliorer les pratiques de RSE au sein de l'entreprise, au regard de considérations sociales.

Le cas Mafelec

Mafelec est fabricant de matériel électrique. En 2003, afin de répondre à une demande de baisse du coût de son donneur d'ordre Schneider, alors actionnaire majoritaire, la direction décide de délocaliser l'activité en Inde avec une implantation sur un site existant de l'actionnaire majoritaire. En 2008, à la suite du désengagement de Schneider et de problèmes de qualité (traces de radioactivité dans les composants exportés d'Inde), Mafelec relocalise l'activité assemblage en Isère.

Tableau 5.2 Diagnostic de la relocalisation de l'entreprise Mafelec

Forces	Faiblesses
+ Mise en place de la méthode Lean Manufacturing + Amélioration des processus pour une meilleure rentabilité + Une structure « Etudes spécialisées » est créée, 3 personnes travaillent à plein temps sur les processus et l'opportunité de mettre en place des automates. + Maîtrise et préservation du savoir-faire + Budget de R&D plus important + Etude pour le développement d'une nouvelle gamme de produits afin de renouveler le design.	- Charges plus importantes
Opportunités	**Menaces**
+ Rationalisation du travail qui permet de baisser les coûts de production + Investissement dans des automates + Diminution des délais et des coûts de transport	- Législation protégeant les salariés plus contraignante que la législation indienne

Ainsi, MAFELEC Mafelec abandonne sa stratégie de différenciation par les coûts pour adopter une stratégie de différenciation de ses produits vers le haut de gamme, en proposant des produits avec une meilleure finition et une qualité renforcée. La délocalisation a eu un impact quantitatif sur les effectifs : suppression d'une vingtaine de contrats précaires sur des emplois peu qualifiés sans que ceci ne s'accompagne de restructuration ou de plan social. Le mouvement de relocalisation a eu un impact qualitatif sur les emplois : création de 3 postes de techniciens maintenance et 2 au bureau d'étude en lien avec les investissements d'automates ainsi que 2 postes d'opérateurs spécialisés dans la surveillance des automates. L'investissement en automate donne une capacité de production supérieure à celle réalisée en Inde par des opérateurs, pour un coût financier peu élevé. Les collectivités locales et territoriales n'ont été sollicitées pour aucune des deux étapes.

Le cas Smoby

Smoby est une entreprise de jouets, originaire du Jura, dont l'activité est en partie située dans l'Ain. La société commence à fabriquer des produits dans les pays à bas coûts dans les années 1995, afin de pouvoir garder des prix compétitifs tout en continuant à se développer. Depuis 2009, suite à des difficultés rencontrées avec les fournisseurs chinois, et à un manque de réactivité qui en a découlé, Smoby a décidé de produire certaines de ses nouvelles productions en France plutôt qu'en Chine.

Tableau 5.3 Diagnostic de la relocalisation de l'entreprise Smoby

Forces	Faiblesses
+ Position dominante en France et en Europe. + Besoin de proximité avec ses clients. + Réinvestissement dans l'outil de production en France.	- Relations clients-fournisseurs difficiles. - Délais de livraison trop longs : impossibilité de réapprovisionnements rapides.
Opportunités	**Menaces**
+ Amélioration de l'outil de production. + Diminution des délais et des coûts de transport.	- Peu de fiabilité des entreprises locales. - Manque de main d'œuvre qualifiée - Augmentation des salaires - Augmentation du prix des matières premières. - Manque de confiance dans les fournisseurs asiatiques. - Augmentation du prix des transports. - Les consommateurs recherchent du « Made in France » pour les jouets.

Ainsi, pour l'entreprise c'est un atout que d'avoir une production de proximité avec des délais de livraison courts sur ses principaux marchés que constituent la France et l'Europe, ce qui représente un avantage face à des concurrents chinois ou américains. L'entreprise SMOBY souhaite ainsi baisser l'impact de la saisonnalité sur les produits : aujourd'hui 60% de la production se fait à Noël. Elle communique beaucoup sur le fait de vouloir ainsi **conserver l'emploi en France**.

Suite au mouvement de délocalisation, la société SMOBY n'a jamais eu recours à des plans sociaux. L'objectif de la délocalisation était surtout de développer une nouvelle production à l'étranger qui n'existait pas en France. Ainsi aucune production en France n'a été arrêtée. Cependant, le développement économique et la création d'emplois qui ont eu lieu à l'étranger se sont faits au détriment de la création d'emplois en France dans un souci de rentabilité. Ainsi même si l'effectif a été réduit, ces suppressions ont fait l'objet d'une bonne gestion de l'emploi :

- Départ à la retraite non remplacé ;
- Départ volontaire non remplacé ;
- Développement des compétences.

Les collectivités locales n'ont jamais aidé l'entreprise pour garder l'emploi ou éviter le départ de nouveaux jouets en Chine. Toutefois, la délocalisation n'a pas eu que des impacts négatifs sur l'emploi : certains postes ont dû être créés ou préservés grâce à la fabrication dans les pays à bas coût : il a fallu faire des suivis de projet, des expatriés ont été envoyés en Chine, de nouveaux fournisseurs chinois ont été approchés. Mais, il faut souligner l'impact important de la série d'acquisitions qui a engendré un lourd endettement : des suppressions d'emplois conséquentes au cours de l'année 2008 en France : 396 personnes ont été licenciées. Actuellement, la politique de ressources humaines en France consiste à :

- augmenter les compétences des salariés surtout sur les nouveaux matériels utilisés.
- travailler sur l'ergonomie (fabrication de grosses pièces)
- recruter du personnel compétent et à potentiel, pouvant faire marcher ces nouvelles machines

Le cas PCI SCEMM

PCI SCEMM (126 salariés en 2010) est une filiale à 99,9% du groupe PSA dont 90% (fabrication de machines-outils destinées aux constructeurs automobile et équipementiers de l'automobile) est destinée à PSA. Vers le milieu des années 2000, face à une situation économique difficile (forte baisse du chiffre d'affaires et mise en place de plans sociaux), la direction délocalise en 2006 l'activité de tables d'usinage, d'armoires électriques, de construction de bâtis auprès de sous-traitants en République Tchèque et en Pologne, et de manière plus marginale en Espagne.

En 2008, face à l'augmentation des coûts de production des sous-traitants tchèques et polonais, de problèmes liés au délai et à la qualité des produits, la direction relocalise ces productions auprès de sous-traitants Rhône-alpins. Les armoires électriques sont produites par un sous-traitant situé dans l'Ain, et les tables d'usinage par des sous-traitants ligériens.

Tableau 5.4 : Diagnostic de la relocalisation de PCI SCEMM

Forces	Faiblesses
+ Accès au changement technique + Intégration à un pôle de compétitivité	- Accès à des marchés extérieurs
Opportunités	**Menaces**
+ Sensibilité au taux de change moins importante. + Facilité d'insertion de réseaux territoriaux inter-entreprises.	- Evolution du différentiel de coût

Ainsi, grâce à la relocalisation, les transferts de compétences et la coordination avec les sous-traitants sont facilités par la proximité géographique et linguistique. **Cette décision a conduit d'ailleurs à l'embauche de 4 salariés après 10 ans de baisse des effectifs.**

De nos quatre cas étudiés, il ressort que ce sont essentiellement des raisons liées aux coûts, souvent sous-estimés, qui justifient les relocalisations. En effet, il ne suffit pas de prendre en compte les coûts liés au salaire, qui peuvent tendre à augmenter, mais également, les coûts de transport, les délais de livraison… tous les coûts liés à l'éloignement. Il est donc indispensable de raisonner à coût complet en tenant compte des coûts de coordination notamment liés à la distance géographique. Un autre argument semble être prédominant : la qualification de la main d'œuvre, qui favorise la créativité et la maîtrise du savoir-faire de l'entreprise. Ainsi, l'entreprise peut mieux adapter son produit aux exigences de la clientèle. Un autre aspect est mis en avant : la possibilité de faciliter le travail en réseau et ainsi la coopération entre tous les acteurs liés à l'activité de l'entreprise du fait de leur proximité.

Au final, on remarque, que même s'il est fait état par le biais des médias, d'une volonté des dirigeants de favoriser leur responsabilité vis-à-vis de la société et de mettre en place de nouvelles pratiques de RSE, il nous apparaît que la RSE s'explique a postériori, une fois que la décision de relocaliser a été prise, mais qu'elle n'est pas à la base de cette décision. Les pratiques de RSE, au regard de considérations sociales ne constitue pas le fondement de la décision de relocaliser les activités en France.

Enfin aucune de ces quatre entreprises n'a bénéficié d'aide des pouvoirs publics. Et pourtant, le mouvement des relocalisations est largement plébiscité par les pouvoirs publics français. Sa prise en compte est apparu lors des derniers Etats Généraux de l'Industrie, dont le rapport final du 1er février 2010 stipule certes, une volonté de renforcer la performance à l'export des entreprises françaises, et notamment des PME, mais également souligne l'importance de la mise en place d'un dispositif en faveur de relocalisations compétitives, et donc de favoriser l'ancrage territorial des PME en France.

Cet ancrage devrait permettre de freiner la désindustrialisation de l'économie française et relancer la croissance en France. D'où une multitude de mesures en faveur de ce mouvement dont la prime à la relocalisation, qui a été transformée en prime à la réindustrialisation et la création d'un label « origine France » qui permet aux consommateurs de différencier les produits et de privilégier « l'achat citoyen ». Mais on peut s'interroger des conséquences de ces mesures sur l'emploi ?

3. Les mesures mises en place en faveur des relocalisations renforcent-elles les pratiques de RSE de la PME ?

Les mesures actuellement mises en place en faveur des relocalisations sur le territoire d'origine nous semblent avoir un effet assez limité dans la mesure où elles n'ont pas d'impact direct sur l'emploi. Elles visent effectivement à faire revenir les entreprises, mais leur objectif en termes de création d'emplois n'est pas ou très peu précisé. Depuis les années 1980, en France, les gouvernements successifs ont tenté d'enrayer le départ des entreprises françaises. Le gouvernement français actuel a fait du combat pour que «*l'on garde des usines en France*»; l'un de ses thèmes de prédilection. L'appel à la relocalisation des usines et à la défense de la production industrielle fut un des thèmes majeurs de la campagne électorale pour la Présidence de 2012.

Tous les candidats défendent « *une grande politique de relocalisation des productions* ». Ainsi, le gouvernement français propose une succession de mesures spécifiques pour favoriser la relocalisation des entreprises françaises. Nous pouvons citer :

- **Le crédit d'impôt à la relocalisation** (mis en place par Jean-Pierre Raffarin et entré en vigueur du 01/01/2005 au 31/12/2006) ;
- **La prime à la relocalisation** (mise en place en 2010, la première entreprise bénéficiaire a été la fonderie Loiselet). L'objectif de cette prime était d'aider 30 à 40 entreprises de moins de 5 000 salariés en leur accordant une aide remboursable. L'enveloppe globale était de

200 millions d'euros, remboursable sur une période de trois ans et demi.

Afin d'être éligible pour la demande d'aide au financement de la relocalisation, l'entreprise devait respecter les trois conditions suivantes :

1. avoir un ou des projets d'investissements d'au moins 5 millions d'euros,
2. créer au moins 25 emplois permanents,
3. tout cela dans un délai maximum de 36 mois.

C'est seulement cette aide conditionnelle qui explicite clairement l'objectif de la création d'emplois. Il convient de signaler, dans ce contexte, que **la création d'un label « origine France »** est entrée en vigueur le 19/05/2011. L'intérêt du label est d'apporter une information claire et garantie sur l'origine des produits, d'encourager la production voire la relocalisation en France. Il est accordé, aux entreprises qui en font la demande, par le Bureau Veritas Certification. Pour l'obtenir[5], il faut qu'au moins 50% de la valeur d'un produit soit acquise sur le territoire national ; en outre, le ou les lieux où le produit a pris ses caractéristiques essentielles doit être situé en France.

Ainsi, les moyens qui sont mis en place, actuellement, par les pouvoirs publics français, semblent bien dérisoires par rapport aux besoins qu'a la PME pour relocaliser ses activités sur son territoire d'origine au regard de considérations sociales (embauche de salariés sur le territoire d'origine, formation de ces derniers) et sociétales (développement d'une production respectueuse de l'environnement, contribution aux dépenses collectives via le paiement de l'impôt en France). Pour que la PME quitte le territoire d'accueil et assume sa responsabilité sociétale sur son territoire d'origine, il faudrait qu'elle obtienne davantage de soutien de la part des pouvoirs publics en faveur de l'emploi, qu'un empilement de mesures comme celles décrites précédemment.

Conclusion

Ainsi comme Azam et al. (2007, p.67) qui indiquent que la relocalisation des activités économiques renvoie à l'idée d'une économie comme « *moyen au service des besoins humains, et non plus d'une économie obéissant à la seule logique de la rentabilité, considérant le territoire comme simple lieu géographique et support d'activités dont le but est ailleurs* », nous avons étudié des cas de PME qui relocalisaient

[5] Il existe un site internet dédié à ce label : http://www.madein-france.com

pour savoir dans quelle mesure un déterminant de cette stratégie relevait d'un comportement socialement responsable.

Il nous apparait qu'une des conséquences des relocalisations est bien la création d'emplois aussi modeste soit-elle dans certains cas. Cependant, la création d'emplois en France n'est pas un déterminant de la relocalisation ; il s'agit plutôt de la hausse des coûts liés à l'éloignement, de la baisse de la qualité et de la moindre réactivité de l'entreprise qui explique la relocalisation d'activité. C'est une fois revenue, que l'entreprise va gérer les ressources humaines et communiquer sur sa RSE. Mais la relocalisation ne nous semble pas être une pratique de RSE, dans le pays d'origine, en tant que telle. Enfin les actuelles mesures mises en place par les autorités publiques en faveur des relocalisations ne sont pas directement liées à l'emploi, même si in fine, il s'agit bien de relancer l'emploi avec le retour d'activités délocalisées. Peut-être serait-il préférable, en complément des mesures actuelles, d'accompagner les entreprises dans leur démarche de mobilité par une politique fiscale favorable et de renforcer durablement l'attractivité du territoire, en soutenant la recherche, et en investissant dans la formation.

Bibliographie

Allemand, S. (2005), *Les nouveaux utopistes de l'économie*, Editions Autrement Frontières, Paris, 255 p.

Acquier, A., Aggeri, F. (2007), « Une généalogie de la pensée managériale sur la RSE », *Revue française de gestion*, 2007/11, N°180, p. 131-157.

Azam, G. et al. (2007), « Construire un monde écologique et solidaire », L'Économie Politique, 2007/2 n°34, p.60-71.

Bouba-Olga, O. (2006), Les nouvelles géographies du capitalisme. Comprendre et maitriser les délocalisations, Le Seuil.

Bouveret-Rivat, C. et Mercier-Suissa, C. (2010), *PME : Conquérir des parts de marché à l'international,* Dunod, collection Entreprendre, 224 p.

Calof, JL. (1993), « The impact of size on internationalization », *Journal of Small Business Management*, n°31, pp.60-69.

—. (1994), « The relationship between firm size and export behavior revisited », *Journal of International Business Studies*, n°25, p. 367-387.

CEDRE, Ifop (2011), « Le Made in France – Regards croisés Français et chef d'entreprise », Paris.

Chanteau, J.P. (2008), « Quantification et analyse stratégique des délocalisations », *Revue d'Economie industrielle*, n°124, déc. p.23-50.

Chanteau, J.P. et Mercier-Suissa C. (sous la dir.) (2011), « Délocalisation d'Activités et Mobilité Internationale des Entreprises en Rhône-Alpes », projet DAMIER, rapport final 4 juin 2011, projet Cible 2009, rendu à la Région Rhône-Alpes, juin 2011, 38 p.

Grolleau G., Lakhal, T. et Mzoughi, N. (2004), « Does Ethical Activism Lead to Firm Relocation », *Kyklos*, vol.57, Fasc. 3, p.387-402.

Gasmi, N. et Grolleau, G. (2002), « Les risques d'effets pervers des opérations de délocalisation par acquisition », *Revue Humanisme et Entreprise*, octobre, p.41-47.

Liesch P.W. et Knight, G. A. (1999), « Information, internalization and hurdle rates in SME internationalization », *Journal of International Business Studies*, n°30 p. 383–394.

Mercier-Suissa, C. (sous la dir.) (2011), Entre délocalisations et Relocalisation : mobilité des entreprises et attractivité des territoires, Karthala, Les terrains du siècle, 247 p.

—. (2009), « RSE et sous-traitance dans les pays à bas coûts », in *Indicateurs d'évaluation de la responsabilité sociale et environnementale des entreprises*, 8-10 Juin 2009, Lyon, Université Jean Moulin Lyon 3, France organisé en partenariat entre l'ISEOR et l'Academy of Management (Etats-Unis), Tome II, p.1151-1163.

Mercier-Suissa C. et J. Belbenoit Avich, (2009), «Rôle des parties prenantes dans la décision de relocalisation », colloque *À la recherche de l'intention - L'imagination au service de la Gestion*, ESC Brest, 29 et 30 janvier 2009, p. 29.

Mercier-Suissa C. et Bouveret-Rivat C., (2008), « Délocalisation ou innovation organisationnelle dans le pays d'origine - Faut-il délocaliser ? », XVIIIème Congrès de l'AISLF, Istanbul, 7-11 juillet 2008, 24 p.

Mouhoud, E.M. (2006), *Mondialisation et délocalisation des entreprises*, La Découverte, collection Repères, 122 p.

Trautmann, F. (2004), « Pourquoi boycotter ? Logique collective et expressions individuelles : analyse de systèmes de représentations à partir du cas Danone », *Le Mouvement Social*, 2004/2 n° 207, p. 39-55.

ENJEUX ET CONSEQUENCES DE LA LRU ET LA RCE SUR LA GOUVERNANCE UNIVERSITAIRE : LE CAS DE L'UNIVERSITE DE LA ROCHELLE

NEHMÉ AZOURY, JEAN-YVES DUYCK AND MARIO SASSINE

Résumé

L'objectif de cet article consiste à se focaliser sur les enjeux et les conséquences de la LRU (Libertés et Responsabilités des Universités) et de son impact sur le fonctionnement et le développement de l'université publique française en général, et celle de La Rochelle en particulier. Depuis le vote de la LRU et la RCE (Responsabilités et Compétences élargies) en Août 2007, divers établissements académiques font face à une multitude de problématiques. Les budgets globaux, leur fongibilité, la responsabilisation des personnels et l'entrée dans de nouvelles formules d'allocations incitatives en interne deviennent la règle d'une part. D'autre part, la différenciation interuniversitaire questionne les moyens d'acquisition de compétences auxquelles les universités ont de plus en plus recours pour répondre aux exigences d'une concurrence académique. Ces deux volets, bien qu'ils soient complémentaires, demeurent au cœur des préoccupations et des orientations stratégiques de la gouvernance universitaire.

Mots-Clés : Autonomie, gouvernance universitaire, compétences, budget financier, savoir, capital humain, ressources humaines, recrutement, présidentialisme, pouvoir.

Abstract

The aim of this paper is to focus on the issues and the consequences of the LRU and its impact on the development of the public French universities in general, and the one of La Rochelle in particular. Since the vote of the LRU and the RCE in August 2007, various academic institutions were facing a multitude of problematic. Global budgets, their fungibility, accountability of the personnel, entry into new forms of incentive allowances become internally the rule on one hand. On the other hand, the differentiation between universities interrogates the means of acquiring specific skills to which the universities have increasingly resorted to meet the requirements for an academic competition. These two components, although complementary, remain at the heart of the concerns and strategic directions of the university governance.

Keywords: Autonomy, university governance, skills, financial budget, knowledge, human capital, human resources, recruitment, presidentialism, power.

Introduction

LRU, LMD, RCE, RGPP[1], ces termes et le concept d'autonomie qui les accompagne, traduisent un bouleversement de la conception de la gouvernance des universités, et au-delà du paysage universitaire français *via* une conception managériale de sa gestion. Ainsi, l'université française a vu, en moins de dix ans (Cohen, 2009), son statut évoluer vers une plus grande professionnalisation avec l'apparition (puis la disparition) des IUP[2], l'intégration des filières recherche (master recherche) au sein des ex-DESS devenus masters professionnels, etc. Cette refondation de l'université[3] remet en cause la tradition des « humanités » face à une rationalité « managériale », et fragilise *ipso facto* le service public avec une entrée dans des logiques concurrentielles et une remise en question des statuts des enseignants-chercheurs, via la modulation des services, mais aussi de celle des IATOS qui peuvent se voir imposer une mobilité forcée. Ces quelques exemples coïncident depuis 2003, avec un gel de crédits de recherche et avec des suppressions de postes.

Dans cette optique, les manifestations de chercheurs et d'universitaires expriment leur inquiétude sur le devenir de leur métier et aussi sur leur

[1] Si l'on rajoute les Labex, Equipex, Idex, c'est un véritable lexique qu'il faudrait créer pour suivre la logique des classements de Shanghai.

[2] Les Instituts Universitaires Professionnalisés (créés par le décret n° 92-85 du 23 janvier 1992, modifié en 1994) avec un titre d'ingénieur maître et une formation à la recherche)

[3] Le 8ème et dernier des Grands Débats de l'EHESS a eu pour thème la question de la « refondation de l'université ».

carrière académique. D'une part, la divergence de fond sur les orientations incite les chercheurs à réclamer davantage des moyens. D'autre part, le pouvoir met en cause la lourdeur du système de recherche et son incapacité à contribuer de façon efficace au progrès scientifique et technologique. Partant de ces constatations et déplorant l'absence *d'une véritable réforme de l'université,* les différents acteurs se réfugient dans des stratégies défensives. L'autonomie des universités est contestée par différents acteurs selon la question concernée : par les familles à cause du risque d'augmentation des droits d'inscription, par les syndicats du fait du manque de moyens et du système de gouvernance, par l'État à propos de la propriété des bâtiments et par les enseignants-chercheurs au sujet de la modulation des services (ANDèS, 2007).

En France, les universités publiques ont toujours fonctionné sur un modèle collégial et démocratique instauré par la loi de 1984. De ce point de vue, le mode de gouvernance installé par la loi relative aux libertés et responsabilités des universités (LRU appelée aussi loi Pécresse), change fondamentalement le système de gouvernance des universités françaises et aussi le statut des enseignants-chercheurs. Instaurée le 10 Août 2007 pour donner aux universités plus d'autonomie financière et de moyens selon leur performance, cette loi est combattue par ses opposants qui dénoncent la marchandisation des savoirs et la concurrence entre établissements qu'elle provoque. Fondée sur un modèle de gouvernance des établissements s'inspirant d'une logique entrepreneuriale, la LRU constitue un changement paradigmatique radical dans la mesure où elle crée un pouvoir présidentiel au détriment du rôle des différents conseils (CEVU (Conseil des Etudes et de la Vie Universitaire), CS (Conseil Scientifique) et même le CA (Conseil d'Administration). Elle prévoit la généralisation des responsabilités et compétences élargies (RCE) s'appuyant sur l'autonomie budgétaire et de la GRH (Gestion Des Ressources Humaines) au sein des universités.

Au 1er janvier 2009 (cf. annexe 1), dix-huit universités ont souhaité le passage aux RCE dont douze possèdent une faculté de médecine et d'odontologie. Au 1er janvier 2010, trente-trois universités suivront dont dix-sept *dito*[4]. À ce titre, la question de recherche du présent article consiste à savoir dans quelle mesure la LRU constitue un levier approprié pour une gestion efficiente de l'université ? Autrement dit, quel *bonus* ou quel *malus* cette loi a-t-elle engendré depuis son entrée dans le système universitaire? Elle s'appuie sur l'exemple d'une des premières et des plus

[4] Angers, Besançon, Bordeaux, Brest, Dijon, Grenoble, Lille, Nantes, Nice, Paris 11, Paris 12, Paris 13, Poitiers, Rennes, Toulouse, Tours, Versailles.

petites universités y ayant accédé: l'Université de La Rochelle (ULR).

1. De la gouvernance universitaire

Un bref historique de la gouvernance universitaire est réalisé au regard du concept d'autonomie des universités (1.1.). Par ailleurs et avec l'émergence récente du concept de la gouvernance d'entreprise, il importe d'examiner ce dernier dans le contexte universitaire (1.2.). Pour ce faire, il apparaît adéquat de se baser sur les esquisses théoriques du modèle managérial (1.3.) afin de mieux exhiber les enjeux qu'encourt actuellement la gouvernance universitaire (1.4.). À travers cette optique théorique, l'illustration sera avancée aussi à la suite de l'examen de l'interaction et de l'influence des divers conseils composant le système de gouvernance de l'université (1.5.).

Bref historique sur l'évolution de la gouvernance universitaire

Pour Charles et Verger (2007 : 5) :

> *« Chaque époque a dû résoudre le dilemme renaissant de la préservation du savoir passé et de l'intégration de l'innovation, de l'évaluation des compétences et du changement des critères d'appréciation. »*

Cette phrase par laquelle s'achève la préface de leur *Histoire des universités* de résume les tensions auxquelles les universités ont dû faire face depuis le Moyen-âge. L'application de la LRU et la RCE à l'ensemble des universités françaises peut être interprétée aujourd'hui comme le fondement et la prémisse d'un changement, caractérisé par l'octroi d'une « dose d'indépendance » concernant les réflexions stratégiques des établissements quant à la mobilisation de moyens financiers de la part de ces derniers.

Du LMD[5] à la LRU, en passant par le PRES, l'ANR, les RTRA et le Plan Campus, le système d'enseignement supérieur et de recherche français connaît depuis cinq ans une succession d'importantes réformes. Par ailleurs et depuis, ce cadre règlementaire a évolué sans qu'il ne traduise réellement le concept d'autonomie par une véritable indépendance

---

[5] Avec la réforme LMD, la France est entrée depuis 2002 dans une vaste réorganisation de tout l'enseignement supérieur. L'objectif est de permettre la « mobilité » et « l'employabilité » des individus partout en Europe. Aujourd'hui Licence / Master / Doctorat, est l'architecture commune pour les cursus et les diplômes européens.

financière et de gestion. Loin d'être une réforme de rupture, l'adoption de la LRU n'a fait que prolonger les évolutions initiées par Edgar Faure dans le sillage de mai 1968[6]. En effet, la gouvernance actuelle repose sur deux piliers majeurs, légués par la loi Savary de 1984 : l'uniformité[7] et la polysynodie[8]. Cependant et grâce à la loi Faure, les liens entre l'université et la collectivité sont précisés, alors qu'il appartiendra à la loi Savary d'opérer une unification des corps enseignants et une unification des doctorats. De progressions en replis, ces réformes ont significativement modifié la physionomie de l'université publique, par le renforcement des moyens financiers, l'autonomie budgétaire, la constitution de pôles d'excellence, une esquisse d'intégration des grandes écoles et des universités, la création d'agences de moyens en sus des grands organismes de recherche ; enfin, le resserrement des liens entre la recherche innovation et les entreprises dans les pôles de compétitivité. À l'heure actuelle et depuis la mise en œuvre de la LRU et la RCE en 2007, les universités françaises ont été conviées à un important chantier visant à renouveler les perspectives d'avenir de l'institution et du paysage universitaire.

Ce changement se caractérise par l'autonomie financière et la gestion des universités concernées. Plus précisément, les universités bénéficieront d'une grande liberté dans la définition de leur mode d'organisation interne (Laurent, 2006). Par ailleurs, et afin d'atteindre les finalités de cette loi, la

---

[6] Le principe de cogestion, mis en œuvre dans la loi de 1968 relative à l'enseignement supérieur, définit les modalités d'administration des universités ainsi que la représentation de leurs membres au sein des conseils. La cogestion s'organise entre enseignants, chercheurs, personnels administratifs et étudiants. En ce sens, la propriété publique répond au principe d'efficience, les fonctions décisionnelles étant co-localisées au niveau des individus susceptibles de les exercer le plus pertinemment possible (Charreaux, 1994).

[7] Le premier commande que, quelle que soit la nature de l'établissement, sa personnalité, les singularités de son histoire et de son environnement ou le degré de son rayonnement ; son organisation et son financement résultent d'une multitude de textes réglementaires, applicables de la même manière à des universités à dominante littéraire comme Paris-IV Sorbonne, qu'à l'université de Toulouse-III à dominante scientifique et médicale ou à une université insulaire comme celle de Corte.

[8] La polysynodie se traduit, elle, par la superposition d'une multiplicité de conseils élus (conseil d'UFR, CA, CS, CEVU) qui, selon les cas, « assistent » ou « encadrent » l'autorité exécutive qu'est le président. En leur sein, les organisations syndicales, qu'il s'agisse des enseignants, des personnels IATOS (personnel non-enseignant) ou des étudiants, occupent une place de choix en raison d'un mode d'élection conçu pour favoriser leur présence.

restructuration organisationnelle se manifeste à travers la modulation des moyens budgétaires, financiers, de recrutements, de recherche et d'enseignement. Dans cet esprit de réorganisation, chaque établissement nécessite une gestion différenciée, personnalisée, individualisée des personnels qui doit être assurée par les établissements et la nécessaire reconnaissance de la diversité des carrières (Laurent, 2006). Dans cet esprit, il serait perspicace d'examiner les capacités d'adaptation des universités face aux changements profonds que cause l'application de la LRU, et ce en optant pour un système de gouvernance judicieux.

L'approche de la gouvernance au sein du système universitaire

Caby et Hirigoyen (2001) définissent la gouvernance comme étant une manière de conduire, d'éclairer, de diriger les activités d'un groupe de personne. Les critères essentiels d'une bonne gouvernance sont la clarté, la responsabilisation, l'objectivité, la vision sur le long terme et la stratégie. En effet, un mode de gouvernance spécifique à chaque entreprise est élaboré en vue de répondre à des finalités expectatives des parties prenantes.

À l'heure actuelle, les gouvernements de la plupart des pays occidentaux ont invité les universités à créer de nouvelles formations et à mettre en place des nouveaux programmes d'études du premier, second et troisième cycle. Pour cela, il s'avère important de mieux comprendre la gouvernance universitaire dans le but d'améliorer et de valoriser la qualité de l'enseignement supérieur et de la recherche et de réagir face à une demande croissante de responsabilisation (Chamberlain et *al.*, 1993).

Dans cet esprit, les universités ne sont pas exclues d'une telle logique d'évolution dans la mesure où ces dernières sont opérationnelles dans un environnement basé sur une économie de connaissance et de savoir. Ces universités font l'objet depuis une dizaine d'années d'une concurrence exacerbée qui se traduit par une augmentation très importante du nombre de diplômes et de diplômés dans les universités privées.

La réussite des réformes entreprises, en matière de gouvernance et d'amélioration de la gestion des établissements, conditionnent l'approfondissement de l'autonomie des universités et leur capacité à faire face aux nouveaux défis auxquels elles sont confrontées, dans un contexte de concurrence internationale accrue. Si l'on admet le paradigme libéral des bienfaits de la concurrence, un rapprochement des universités publiques d'un modèle international « en leur donnant l'autonomie qui est déjà la règle dans tous les grands pays scientifiques du monde » (Méla, 2008) devient concevable.

Ainsi, les universités publiques sont incitées à devenir flexibles et dotées d'une certaine veille stratégique afin de survire à la concurrence universitaire actuelle et de maintenir un engagement fondé sur la qualité de l'enseignement et de la recherche, et d'insuffler par là une véritable culture d'établissement. Afin d'être en symbiose avec son environnement externe et d'évoluer en fonction des changements effectués par ses homologues pour maintenir sa compétitivité, l'université « moderne » doit prouver son autonomie, son impartialité et sa promesse à l'égard de la création et du transfert objectifs des connaissances.

En effet, il s'agit du passage d'un gouvernement académique à un gouvernement plus ouvert sur l'extérieur, essayant d'incorporer les différentes parties prenantes (Musselin, *in* ANDèS, 2007). Dans ce sens, l'université « moderne » doit prouver aussi son engagement nationale, voire internationale.

La gouvernance universitaire selon le substrat théorique du modèle managérial

En considérant que les intérêts entre les groupes peuvent être divergents et que le CA est une instance politique, la diversité des intérêts représentés doit être encadrée pour assurer la prépondérance des professeurs et des étudiants au lieu de créer un système de règle qui assure, volontairement ou non, l'hégémonie du monde des affaires sur les CA universitaires. Partant de ce cas de figure, chaque agent est supposé poursuivre ses propres objectifs de façon à maximiser sa fonction d'utilité.

L'émergence des organisations à but non lucratif peut être expliquée par la présence de coûts de transaction et de contrôle élevés (Fama et Jensen, 1983). Les agents sont réputés opportunistes[9] au sens de Williamson (1975). Ainsi l'élargissement du cadre théorique contractuel permet alors d'intégrer à la fois la latitude décisionnelle des présidents des universités vis-à-vis des divers conseils et syndicats, mais également un certain nombre de parties prenantes.

La théorie de l'agence constitue ainsi un des principaux champs d'analyse pour l'étude de l'incidence des conflits entre actionnaires et dirigeants (Jensen et Meckling, 1976 ; Fama et Jensen, 1983). *« Gouverner une université française »*, c'est essayer de trouver un équilibre entre les

---

[9] Les comportements de triche, de mensonge et de distorsion volontaire de l'information ne sont pas exclus.

filières juxtaposées: administrative[10], élective[11], délibérative[12] et qui doivent essayer de collaborer (Musselin, *in* ANDèS, 2007).

Dans le cas de la gouvernance universitaire, et plus précisément en tenant compte du rapport entre la composition du CA et le président de l'établissement, l'université peut être amenée à servir des intérêts individuels[13]. Le CA s'ouvre davantage aux personnalités extérieures[14] à l'université et au monde socio-économique. Le CA est investi d'un pouvoir politique dans la mesure où un sentiment de privatisation de l'université peut être perçu. En effet, la prépondérance d'administrateurs professionnels est problématique étant donné que les méthodes de gestion du secteur privé ne sont pas aisément transférables dans le milieu académique puisque les missions des entreprises et les institutions du savoir sont considérablement différentes. Aussi, il importe de souligner que le même intérêt n'est pas partagé pour le devenir des universités. Les décisions stratégiques engendrent des conflits d'intérêt, *« les principales décisions stratégiques étant habituellement subordonnées aux orientations de politique économique définies par les pouvoirs publics ainsi qu'aux contraintes budgétaires »* (Charreaux, 1997). Dès lors la gouvernance universitaire est examinée selon les rapports entre le CA et le président, et analysée aussi sous l'optique des intérêts et les considérations individuels (administrateurs - président), et ce à travers les orientations stratégiques entreprises pour le développement de l'université.

L'acquisition par l'université d'une conception « managériale »

Un des premiers axes consiste à organiser les universités comme des entreprises en facilitant le pouvoir de décision du président et du CA. En effet, les décisions du CA sont prises à la majorité absolue et non plus au

---

[10] Services centraux, dans les unités de formation et de recherche.

[11] Responsables élus (président, directeurs d'UFR, de département, enseignants-chercheurs), mais aucun lien hiérarchique n'existe entre ces divers niveaux.

[12] CA, CS, CEVU, conseils d'UFR, conseils de département.

[13] La loi insiste sur l'objectif de professionnalisation des études à travers l'augmentation des relations avec le bassin socio-économique local. Le choix est offert aux investisseurs de financer des diplômes en relation avec leur activité.

[14] La représentation des étudiants et des enseignants chercheurs a été minorée, et à l'inverse la représentation des personnalités extérieures accrue (nommées par le président de l'université). La taille du CA est réduite de 60 à « 20/ 30 personnes » avec une proportion réduite de salariés et d'étudiants et une place plus grande pour les « partenaires extérieurs » (entreprises et collectivités territoriales) nommés par le président.

deux tiers et un quorum d'une moitié d'élu n'est plus nécessaire à la tenue d'un CA. Les choix stratégiques, politiques et budgétaires doivent être pris en CA, en s'appuyant sur les propositions du CS et du CEVU. Toutefois, la taille du CA est divisée par deux, sans préjudice des grands équilibres de la représentation des personnels et des étudiants. Ses compétences sont étendues. Le CA délibère sur la création des UFR et des fondations, il fixe la répartition des emplois, vote le budget, approuve les comptes financiers et le rapport annuel d'activité présenté par le président.

Cette disposition, ajoutée à la possibilité offerte aux présidents de désigner les personnalités extérieures siégeant au CA, cristallise les inquiétudes exprimées par les étudiants en assemblées générales qui y voient le danger d'un *« désengagement financier de l'Etat »* et d'une *« privatisation »* des universités. Blondel (*in* ANDèS, 2007) craint que le lien entre financement et gouvernance ne devienne prépondérant. Comme le souligne Charreaux (1994), bien que les formations nouvellement habilitées doivent généralement fonctionner à budget constant pour leur première année d'existence, l'ouverture de formations nouvelles permet d'obtenir davantage de ressources auprès de l'administration centrale. Par ailleurs et avec la nouvelle configuration du CA, la création d'une offre de formation fait alors intervenir plusieurs acteurs avec des intérêts potentiellement divergents.

Les administrateurs, aussi chefs d'entreprise, qui financent l'activité d'une entreprise et participant à la gouvernance de l'université, privilégieront des formations académiques qui favorisent le développement humain du futur personnel de leurs sociétés. Or, la gouvernance doit contrôler que toutes les missions scientifique, pédagogique et professionnelle de l'enseignement supérieur public sont remplies. De fait, la gouvernance servira des intérêts différents de l'intérêt collectif dans la mesure où leur financement, par le biais des fondations privées, se justifie par l'élaboration de formations d'enseignement supérieur sélectives. À titre explicatif, les projets de loi constituent un autre pas vers la privatisation de « l'économie du savoir », de la marchandisation de l'enseignement supérieur ainsi que vers l'ingérence accrue d'intérêts privés dans la recherche scientifique. Dans une entreprise privée, les administrateurs sont généralement actionnaires et détiennent un intérêt dans la rentabilité de l'entreprise. Cela ferait des universités des lieux de formation professionnelle en vue de répondre aux besoins du marché plutôt que des institutions d'éducation émancipatrice, critiques de la société et axées principalement sur le développement et la transmission des connaissances (CQSU/AFPC/FTQ, 2009). Dans ce sens, une fois engagée, la gestion de l'université sera dictée par la loi du marché.

L'influence des instances de gouvernance sur la vision stratégique de l'université

Avec l'application de la LRU, l'appréhension de la gouvernance universitaire passe par le renforcement d'un processus antidémocratique (1.5.1.) assisté d'un affaiblissement des conseils consultatifs (1.5.2.).

Un présidentialisme affirmé

Toutefois, le principe de co-gestion mis en œuvre dans la loi[15] de 1968, met l'accent sur une autonomie des universités favorisant la décentralisation du processus décisionnel par l'abandon de tout ou partie des fonctions de contrôle décisionnel et d'évaluation qu'exercent habituellement les Pouvoirs publics (Charreaux, 1994). En revanche, la LRU prévoit qu'aucune affectation ne peut être prononcée si le président de l'université émet un avis défavorable motivé. Le président[16] dispose de pouvoirs bien plus étendus qu'actuellement, notamment en matière de recrutement et de gestion des personnels et des finances de l'établissement. Cette loi est donc dysfonctionnelle au sens où elle ne respecte pas le principe de la collégialité (EHESS, 2009).

> *« L'autorité et la légitimité du président sont renforcées sur les composantes de l'établissement et le recrutement des personnels afin d'affirmer son rôle de stratège. Les compétences du président sont élargies. Il s'impose comme l'animateur d'une équipe de direction cohérente et le porteur du projet d'établissement. À cet effet, il est élu à la majorité absolue des membres élus du conseil d'administration pour un mandat d'une durée de quatre ans, renouvelable une fois. »* (Loi du 10 Août 2007, LRU).

Bien que l'appréhension de la gouvernance soit le contrôle des stratégies de l'exécutif, la gouvernance universitaire n'insuffle pas vraiment l'idée du contrôle de ce dernier tant que le pouvoir, détenu entre les mains du Président de l'université, se caractérise par la centralisation de ses décisions.

---

[15] Relative à l'enseignement supérieur.

[16] À titre indicatif, le président de l'université est élu par les seuls membres élus du CA soit 12 à 22 personnes tout au plus (alors qu'actuellement ce sont les membres des trois conseils, soit à l'UJF par exemple, 140 personnes, qui élisent le président).

Un affaiblissement du rôle des conseils

Il est incontestable qu'un large éventail d'intérêts doit être représenté dans un CA afin d'être le plus représentatif possible. Et que l'autonomie va nécessairement de pair avec la responsabilisation et la régulation (Laurent, 2006). Les systèmes de coordination et de contrôle dépendent de la diffusion des fonctions de ratification et de surveillance par lesquelles s'exercent les droits de contrôle. Par ailleurs, cette vision perçue par les professionnels universitaires ne demeure plus une conception servie par la loi en vigueur afin de garantir une efficience organisationnelle. Dans la nouvelle gouvernance, les compétences[17] des trois conseils ont été redéfinies dans un sens consultatif et non plus décisionnel. *In fine,* seul le Président décide.

Avant l'application de la LRU, la fonction de contrôle était confiée à des assemblées (principalement le CA, le CS et le CEVU), constituées majoritairement par les pourvoyeurs de ressources. Dans les établissements universitaires, les discussions vont donc émerger autour du processus de création de valeur, qui passe essentiellement par la création d'une offre de formation (Charreaux, 1994). Avec la réforme universitaire, le CA[18] délibère encore, mais le CS et le CEVU ne possèdent qu'une voix consultative.

À ce titre, le CA devient le seul organe à vocation stratégique. Ainsi, seuls les membres du CA prennent part à l'élection du président, alors qu'auparavant, les membres du CS et du CEVU prenaient aussi part au vote. Comme accompagnement, la LRU prévoit tout un dispositif qui concentre un pouvoir de décision étendu sur un très petit nombre de personnes, sans qu'aucun dispositif de contrôle ou de contre-pouvoir ne puisse contrer les éventuelles dérives autoritaires et les multiples tentations de « clientélisme » qui pourraient en résulter.

Dans la mesure où le pouvoir se trouve concentré entre les mains de l'équipe présidentielle, le contre-pouvoir émanant des divers conseils se résume à une manifestation consultative, le CA n'étant pas tenu de suivre

---

[17] Ces compétences doivent répondre en effet aux intentions réelles de la LRU. Ces intentions se traduisent toutefois par des missions, des compétences, des budgets, des modalités de financement, de gestion et de recrutement qui remettent profondément en cause le statut des universitaires.

[18] Il est admis que le modèle international de gestion des universités comporte un conseil d'administration formé de personnalités de très haut niveau, indépendantes, pas forcément universitaires, qui assurent le pilotage stratégique de l'établissement, attirent les financements, valident les nominations à des hauts postes et qui nomment le président exécutif de l'université.

les avis émis par le CS et le CEVU. Selon Finance (2007), il s'agit en effet d'un ensemble de mesures législatives qui visent finalement à responsabiliser la « tête » de l'établissement au travers du binôme président et CA. Pourtant, même le CA dont le rôle devrait permettre de limiter les décisions du Président non conformes aux objectifs de l'université, et d'accroître la création de valeur n'est pas à l'abri d'un oukase présidentiel[19]. Dans cet esprit, les fonctionnaires voient leur mission s'amenuiser avec la formalisation des réformes émergentes de la loi LRU. Ainsi, leur engagement vis-à-vis de l'université s'atténue alors même que leur source de motivation se basait en quelque sorte sur un volontariat dont la finalité se focalisait sur le service public. Le passage aux RCE peut aggraver certaines dérives.

2. Les problématiques des universités à la lumière du passage aux RCE

Les RCE, en complément des réformes de la LRU, se justifient par l'importance accrue de la connaissance dans les économies actuelles[20] (Andes, 2007). Le couple LRU – RCE positionne les universités dans un esprit de concurrence, dans l'idée qu'elle améliorera la qualité de l'enseignement et procurera une valeur ajoutée aux les formations universitaires. Il s'agit de répondre à une demande croissante d'enseignement supérieur qui se traduit par la recherche de qualifications élevées[21] et un rôle grandissant de l'éducation[22] pour l'accompagner. Ainsi, l'enseignement supérieur constitue un puissant levier de la compétition internationale.

Des pôles universitaires à vocation mondiale cherchent à accueillir les « meilleurs » étudiants et des chercheurs renommés. Les ressources humaines apparaissent comme le domaine le plus concerné par la LRU, avec l'évolution des règles et des pratiques mises en œuvre, mais aussi avec le risque de pénaliser les petites universités qui ne possèdent pas toujours les mêmes moyens financiers.

Une première conséquence de la LRU est le risque du renforcement des inégalités entre universités (Schaub, 2007), et cela tant au niveau du

---

[19] Afin de finaliser ce processus antidémocratique, le président est doté d'une voix prépondérante en cas de litige. Cette première salve de correctifs dessine déjà les nouvelles lignes de force qui vont présider à la tenue des CA.

[20] L'université faisant de la recherche est productrice de savoirs.

[21] L'université offrant des formations diversifiées aux étudiants fait de la diffusion des savoirs.

[22] Le rôle de l'université dans la formation des enseignants.

recrutement d'enseignants qualifiés qu'à celui de leur rémunération. L'université se trouve alors face à une difficulté supplémentaire : assurer à la fois le financement de niveaux d'enseignement et de recherche élevés.

La confrontation de l'université à un dilemme permanent recrutement /budget

Dans le cadre d'un pilotage renforcé, il est proposé aux universités d'adopter ce que l'on appelle de nouvelles compétences. Grâce à l'article 16 de la LRU, l'université et son plus haut représentant, peuvent demander *« à bénéficier de responsabilités et de compétences élargies en matière budgétaire et de gestion des ressources humaines »*. Avec la loi LRU et le transfert des compétences, du budget et de la masse salariale (2.1.1.), l'établissement universitaire demeure relativement limité par les ressources (2.1.2.) que cette loi leur accorde. La RCE inscrit dès lors les établissements académiques dans une optique de concurrence interuniversitaire. Les compétences élargies touchent majoritairement à trois niveaux pour le fonctionnement de l'université (Finance, 2007). Il appartiendra ainsi aux établissements d'en faire de véritables supports de gestion par objectifs :

- celles-ci tournent principalement autour d'une maîtrise globale du budget incluant la maîtrise de la masse salariale ;
- le deuxième type de compétences étendues concerne la maîtrise des RH ;
- enfin, le troisième grand volet de ce bloc de nouvelles compétences concerne l'immobilier et le foncier.

La gestion des emplois et de la masse salariale

Partant des principes « d'économie du savoir » et de l'université comme moteur de développement du « capital humain », cette dernière est souvent confrontée à une problématique budgétaire qui relève d'une stratégie de recherche définie dans le projet de l'établissement. Cette stratégie se focalise en partie sur la question de la légitimité de l'université, en termes de qualité, envers ses parties prenantes et du maintien de cette légitimité avec la question de la dotation financière indispensable au développement académique de l'établissement. Chaque université présente ses propres caractéristiques, aussi bien en matière d'offre de formation (les « maquettes ») que de possibilités pour la recherche. Les éléments de différenciation, tels que l'internationalisation de la formation ou la recherche, prennent par ailleurs de plus en plus d'importance (Charreaux, 1994).

En effet, comme le souligne le rapport de la commission Pineau-Valenciennes (*in* Charreaux, 1994), la compétitivité des entreprises françaises dépend en partie de la qualité des dirigeants et des cadres qui sont formés dans l'enseignement supérieur ainsi que de celle de la recherche en gestion, Ces ressources intangibles, uniques et non substituables, constituent un avantage compétitif. Cependant, le recrutement d'un corps professoral hautement qualifié et des cadres professionnels[23] constitue une difficulté majeure pour l'administration, dans la mesure où ce recrutement nécessite un budget élevé. Sur ce point, l'autonomie, aux yeux des adversaires de la LRU, ne serait que le vecteur de la marchandisation du savoir voulue par l'OCDE et l'UE et de la mise à mort du service public républicain, l'outil d'une université libérale et inégalitaire, la dernière arme contre les libertés de l'enseignant chercheur (Cohen, 2009). Comme le souligne Hélène Machina (2009) :

> *« ce que cache la LRU, c'est d'une part, un très grand retard dans les moyens alloués à la formation supérieure et à la recherche, une volonté de désengagement de l'État à l'égard de ses universités et, d'autre part, la disparition des processus démocratiques et la mise en place d'une concurrence effrénée entre enseignants-chercheurs, laboratoires et facultés ».*

À défaut de trouver des moyens financiers qui contribuent au développement de l'organisation, la LRU autorise les financements privés sous forme de fondations. Plus précisément, une fraction significative du budget des établissements provient du revenu créé par leurs propres actifs, les personnels de l'université sont incités à trouver des moyens, indépendamment de tout soutien financier de la part de l'État afin d'assurer leur pérennité et aussi leur qualité d'enseignement. De fait, la théorie de la stratégie fondée sur les ressources et compétences, issue des recherches de Penrose (1959), cherche à comprendre les facteurs qui orientent et qui conditionnent le développement des universités en termes de recherche et d'enseignement.

Ainsi, les universités auront de plus en plus recours à des fonds auprès de donateurs privés afin de favoriser à terme leur indépendance financière et d'assurer leur qualification académique. À cela s'ajoute une autre possibilité face aux restrictions budgétaires et qui consiste en l'augmentation des frais d'inscription des étudiants. On notera que l'Etat

[23] L'intérêt réside dans le fait de recruter dans des domaines où les compétences sont très recherchées actuellement : gestion du patrimoine immobilier, valorisation et propriété intellectuelle, contrôleur de gestion, informatique…

français s'est assuré une certaine paix sociale vis-à-vis des organisations étudiantes en renonçant à utiliser ce levier[24], mais que certaines universités ont tenté de contourner ces dispositions par l'instauration de « droits spécifiques » régulièrement condamnés par les tribunaux. Dans ce contexte, l'université se transforme en un esprit managérial, à savoir, celui de l'entreprise et selon lequel la mission du service public sera enrayée afin d'être remplacée par la marchandisation du savoir. Adossée à un budget global en pénurie et dans lequel seuls les crédits en direction de la recherche privée augmentent, cette mesure suscite des inquiétudes pour les formations et les recherches qui ne rencontreraient pas les intérêts privés. Les chercheurs y voient le risque de perdre leur indépendance et la logique disciplinaire de recherche. Comme résultante, toutes les universités ne seront pas à égalité dans la recherche de subventions. Une accentuation de la mise en concurrence des universités est perçue.

La gestion des ressources humaines et les fondations privées

La gestion des emplois et de la masse salariale passe par l'élaboration d'un budget financier de la part des universités. On l'a dit, le recrutement de chercheurs réputés présente des difficultés majeures dans la mesure où les universités ne maîtrisent pas la gestion de leurs propres personnels (ANDèS, 2007).

Certains établissements ne peuvent se permettre d'investir de gros budgets dans un capital humain spécifique et distinctif pour la production d'un savoir particulier. Le contexte actuel d'incertitudes et de raréfaction chronique du financement des universités par l'Etat met à mal la continuation des missions de recherche et d'enseignement des universités, la LRU a élargi leurs possibilités de recourir à des fonds privés, notamment par le biais de création de *« fondations universitaires »* dont les ressources proviennent des donations. Ces fondations assurent en partie le recrutement d'enseignants qualifiés pour la transmission d'un savoir à des formations spécifiques. De fait, ces enseignants sont chèrement payés dans la mesure où leur contribution académique reflète la valorisation de la qualité des formations et la création de valeur. Ainsi, les enseignants ne seraient donc plus payés directement par l'État mais par leurs universités, ce qui peut remettre en cause leur statut. Par ponction sur la masse

[24] Il est probable que l'épisode des grèves et des manifestations des jeunes lors du CPE a pesé lourd dans cette décision. Leur absence au moment du mouvement d'opposition à l'allongement de la durée de cotisation pour les retraites en 2010, malgré un niveau de manifestants très levé a probablement été décisive pour le gouvernement.

salariale, le Président peut alors recruter des CDD et CDI à la place de fonctionnaires. Dès lors les établissements auraient la pleine initiative de la gestion de leurs emplois, à titre de création et de suppression de postes bien déterminés, en termes de gestion ou d'enseignement.

3. Le cas de l'université de La Rochelle à la lumière de la LRU

En quinze années d'existence, l'Université de La Rochelle a su s'imposer comme un acteur important de l'enseignement supérieur et de la recherche au niveau régional, national et international. Elle est aujourd'hui confrontée à un nouveau défi, crucial pour son avenir immédiat : l'adaptation à son environnement institutionnel en pleine mutation. Elle va devoir chercher à se renforcer dans la logique politique et territoriale de la création des « Pôles de Recherche et d'Enseignement Supérieur » (PRES).

À cet égard, la création d'un futur PRESCA (PRES Centre Atlantique La Rochelle-Limoges-Poitiers) est fondamentale pour accroître le rayonnement et la visibilité des axes de développement stratégique de cette université.

Par ailleurs, le nouveau cadre organisationnel et réglementaire que constitue la loi « Libertés et Responsabilités des Universités » mérite toute attention, car si les nouvelles compétences qu'elle offre peuvent constituer une réelle chance à saisir, elles n'en demeurent pas moins potentiellement porteuses de risques :

- élargissement des prérogatives du CA et du Président ;
- facilitation du recrutement de personnels contractuels et, dans le même temps, renforcement du pouvoir présidentiel sur les personnels ;
- disparition des commissions de spécialistes élues et formées selon les sections disciplinaires au profit de comités de sélection nommés par le CA ;
- élargissement des compétences de l'établissement en matière de gestion des budgets, des ressources humaines et du parc immobilier.

Posture épistémologique et méthodologie de la recherche

Le choix de la démarche méthodologique et des méthodes de recherche conditionne la qualité du chemin emprunté vers la connaissance. Afin d'asseoir une véritable architecture de recherche, l'orientation méthodologique

(3.1.1.) s'accompagne du choix des méthodes appropriées d'accès au réel (3.1.2.).

Une posture inductive

Plusieurs éléments ont, *de facto*, imposé une posture inductive : 1) l'absence de cadre théorique robuste et des doutes sur la « portabilité » du cadre générique de la gouvernance d'entreprises privées à celui d'universités publiques ; 2) la multiplicité des parties prenantes : enseignants, enseignants-chercheurs, administratifs, mais aussi responsables de filières, d'UFR, étudiants, etc. ; 3) le caractère récent ne donnant pas de recul suffisant pour poser des hypothèses elles aussi robustes. Dès lors, un travail d'analyse du terrain, en profondeur, est apparu nécessaire pour comprendre les enjeux et les conséquences de la nouvelle donne de la gouvernance universitaire.

Méthodologie de la recherche

Il convient d'examiner successivement le recueil (3.1.2.1.) et l'exploitation des données empiriques (3.1.2.2.).

Recueil des données

Compte tenu du faible nombre de recherches réalisées sur le thème de la gouvernance universitaire, neuf entretiens semi-directifs ont permis de mieux comprendre ces enjeux. Ils ont été réalisés auprès des acteurs directement impliqués dans l'élaboration et la mise en œuvre du « programme » LRU : le président et un vice-président[25] ; deux doyens d'UFR ; le secrétaire général ; la DRH ; les trois représentants des syndicats majoritaires, soit chez les enseignants, soit dans le corps des BIATOS. Chaque entretien a duré entre 45 mn et 1h20. Il a semblé, après ces entretiens, avoir atteint le principe de saturation, à savoir qu'un nouvel entretien (par exemple syndical) n'apportait pas d'élément nouveau.

L'exploitation des données

Compte tenu de la nature du matériau de base de cette recherche : du texte, mais aussi du volume global de ces entretiens (75 pages environ), l'exploitation des données a été réalisée par la statistique textuelle grâce au

[25] Il est à noter que l'un des VP n'a pas jugé nécessaire de nous recevoir arguant d'une position identique à celle de son président ; un autre était absent pour plusieurs semaines.

logiciel Alceste 2010. Alceste procède à un classement des « phrases » (dites unités de contexte élémentaire ou u.c.e.) en fonction de la répartition des mots dans ces « phrases », afin de dégager les principaux « mondes lexicaux ». La typologie réalisée est donc interne au corpus (les mondes lexicaux). Elle retrace les « espaces référentiels » investis par l'énonciateur lors de l'élaboration du discours. Les principaux résultats et leur discussion sont proposés ci-après.

Résultats et discussions

Le corpus est exploité à 56% par le logiciel, cette situation signifiant que 44% des discours sont « rejetés » car ne constituant pas un « espace référentiel » au sens d'ALCESTE. Cette situation relativement rare sera explorée lors de la discussion. Par ailleurs le corpus se révèle normé au sens d'un loi de Zipf, mais aussi en termes de richesse de vocabulaire. Le dendrogramme de la classification descendante hiérarchique laisse apparaître 6 classes qui peuvent être regroupées deux par deux (1 et 6 ; 2 et 3 ; 4 et 5). La présentation qui va suivre reprend ces regroupements qui sont caractéristiques d'affinités non fortuites.

Le regroupement n°1 : le discours du service public

Il est typique du discours syndical et possède comme lien principal la crainte de la disparition du service public d'enseignement supérieur et de recherche. Il s'articule autour de deux sous discours : celui des missions (3.2.1.1.) et celui des moyens (3.2.1.2.).

Le sous discours des missions

Le tableau n°1 reprend les formes significatives de ce discours.

Ce discours sur les missions concerne les besoins de l'étudiant (159) et repose sur deux idées : 1) le contenu des cursus est en train de s'appauvrir (enseignement = 25 ; maquettes = 21) ; 2) on peut suspecter la disparition de la mission de service public de l'université par le biais (43) de l'augmentation des droits (29) ou des frais (25) d'inscription (51) ou de chaires type « Alstom » (21)[26].

Les discours types qui illustrent cette situation exposent que « *les maquettes* [vont] *avoir moins d'heures de cours. Donc finalement, la mission de service public de l'université est en train de grosso modo*

[26] Alstom reste un des gros employeurs rochelais et un des financeurs de la Fondation.

disparaitre et beaucoup d'étudiants [vont se] *poser la question* [d'arbitrer entre écoles et université] ou encore que [même si] *« il n'y aura pas d'augmentation des frais d'inscription. [...] en pratique, ce qui se passe c'est que de nombreuses universités sont en train de s'abstraire de cette obligation par le biais de droits spécifiques »*. En outre, *« la LRU conduit à la perte des diplômes nationaux »*.

Tableau 6.1. Formes significatives de la classe 1

Formes	Khi2	Effectif Classe	%
Etudiant	159	44	95%
Inscription	51	16	100%
Biais	43	10	100%
Diplôme	37	16	80%
Ingenieur	34	8	100%
Proximite	30	7	100%
Syndicat	30	71	30%
Droit	29	15	73%
Frais d'inscription14	25	6	100%
enseignement	25	11	71%
LMD	25	6	100%
Ecole	24	11	88%
Réussir	24	7	88%
Science	21	5	100%
Stage	21	5	100%
Université	21	57	32%
Alsthom	21	5	100%
Maquettes	21	6	100%

Bref, dans la mesure où l'Etat n'abonde plus les budgets des universités et réduit le nombre de postes, c'est bien la mission de service public que remet en cause la LRU, tant dans le contenu des diplômes que dans leur financement. Le sous-discours sur les moyens vient compléter les doutes vis-à-vis de la mise en place de la LRU.

Le sous-discours des moyens

Le sous-discours sur les moyens est caractéristique de la classe 6. Il complète la classe 1 sur le fait que la LRU va affecter la dotation en moyens de l'université, en particulier les moyens humains (tableau n°2).

Tableau 6.2 : formes significatives de la classe 6

Formes	Khi2	Effectif Classe	%
Syndicat	69	123	51%
Personnel	31	36	73%
Fonctionnaire	31	24	84%
Poste	31	24	90%
Attendre	25	13	100%
Embaucher	25	14	100%
Prime	24	20	93%
Retrouver	24	13	93%
Salaire	23	16	100%
Forcement	19	12	92%
Carrière	19	10	100%
Humain	17	18	73%
Titulaire	16	12	85%
Retraite	16	16	85%
Compétent	15	16	71%
Gens	14	11	79%
Problème	14	11	79%
Agent	13	8	89%

C'est le manque de personnel (31), en particulier de fonctionnaires (31) qui est en jeu chaque fois que l'on doit embaucher (25) sans pour autant y trouver un bénéfice en termes de salaire (23). On comprend, dans les phrases-types proposées par le logiciel, combien la crainte est grande, en particulier sur les dotations en postes que le service public ne soit remis en question, à la fois compte tenu du travail supplémentaire qui va peser sur les personnels sans compensation salariale : « *ils ne s'attendaient pas à tout ce travail phénoménal. Il a fallu créer des postes, former les gens, je parle au niveau gestion, gestionnaires de l'établissement, qui ont amputé forcement [...] la masse salariale, donc on se retrouve avec des primes qui disparaissent* », et mais aussi du fait de non remplacement des postes : « *on a vraiment des soucis là-dessus. C'est-à-dire qu'avant la LRU, un poste était créé, il était mis au concours, concourraient un certain nombre de personnes qui étaient recrutées en catégorie C, la plus basse jusqu'à la catégorie A* » [nota : avec la LRU les dotations se font sur ressources propres]. S'y ajoute un sentiment de démotivation mais aussi d'iniquité dans la mesure où le partage salarial est perçu comme injuste : « *parce-que maintenant, [...], vous vous rendez compte, on se retrouve avec des salaires phénoménaux, avec des primes phénoménales. En-haut [de la hiérarchie], ils prennent presque 50% à 60% des primes de la masse salariale. Il ne faut pas s'étonner que derrière on ne suit pas ».* Le regroupement n°2 concerne un discours sur les marges de manœuvre.

Le regroupement n°2 : le discours des marges de manœuvre

Les deux discours de ce regroupement proviennent quasi-exclusivement des administratifs, qui dans ce cas précis, sont ceux de l'administration centrale, qui tentent de voir quelles opportunités ou marges de manœuvre la LRU laisse à une petite université comme La Rochelle. Deux effets éléments peuvent être pris en compte, conduisant à deux sous discours : l'effet de taille (3.2.2.1.) et le patrimoine (3.2.2.2.).

Classe 2 : le sous-discours de la taille

Tableau 6.3 formes significatives de la classe 2

Tableau 6.3

Formes	Khi2	Effectif Classe	%
Taille	81	12	83%
administration	61	40	23%
Marge	54	8	73%
Rester	52	11	64%
inconvénients	50	7	86%
Fort	42	6	75%
Matière	42	6	75%
Auto	40	5	100%
Manœuvre	40	5	83%
Capacité	36	9	58%
Gestion	34	17	36%
Capable	33	5	71%
Avantage	33	6	71%
Ordre	30	3	100%
Autonomie	30	15	40%
Faible	28	5	63%
Point	24	5	67%
stratégie16	22	9	46%
Projet	20	4	57%
Servir	20	6	57%

La taille (81) fournit des marges (51) de manœuvre (40), tout en s'avérant aussi un point (24) faible (28). On notera que le terme inconvénients (50) précède largement celui d'avantages 33). Les phrases-types traduisent ces atouts liés à la taille, mais aussi ses faiblesses. Ainsi

« c'est un avantage parce que ça donne une capacité de réactivité qu'aucune autre université que n'ont pas les grosses ; à cette taille-là, on a une capacité aussi à interroger un maximum d'acteurs, à faire participer un maximum d'acteurs à sa stratégie ». A l'opposé : *« donc d'un seul coup, il y a eu une prépondérance extraordinaire de la masse salariale, mais ça reste une petite masse salariale. Donc les marges que l'on peut dégager, elles sont taillées à la hauteur de cette masse salariale; donc ça reste une démarche faible même si en pourcentage, ce n'est pas inintéressant, en volume financier, [...] ça reste modeste.* Et aussi, en matière d'emplois : *« donc peu de mouvements, peu de départs à la retraite. Là aussi, on peut bouger la structure d'emplois, on peut la faire évoluer [...], mais on joue sur une poignée d'emplois vraiment vacants »*.

Au total, l'effet de taille ne semble bien présenter qu'un faible *bonus* proposant un discours optimiste de surface, qui reste cependant lucide en notant les difficultés réelles auxquelles la LRU conduit, si l'on y ajoute la jeunesse de l'université de La Rochelle: autonomie de gestion de l'établissement, certes, mais quasi inexistante sur la gestion des personnels et résistance des personnels tel le 22 mars 2011 menaçant de grève si la mobilité interne était maintenue, et obtenant gain de cause.

Classe 3 : le sous-discours du patrimoine

Le tableau 6.4 regroupe les formes significatives de la classe 3

Le discours sur le patrimoine (38) concerne avant tout les bâtiments (45) dont l'état (28) dépend aussi de l'Etat. Cette marge de manœuvre est double : vendre ou louer les bâtiments, mais cela dépend en grande partie de leur usure, qui en milieu marin, peut s'avérer rapide. La question (23) du contrôle (22), de la maintenance (30), et de l'amortissement (22) se situe donc au cœur de cette problématique.

Actuellement la latitude sur ce sujet reste délicate à déterminer comme en témoignent les réponses-types : *« là il-y-a une vraie question pour laquelle les réponses sont quand-même encore un peu floues globalement, on peut quand-même dire que les bâtiments sont en bon état. Quand on connait l'état du patrimoine des universités françaises, on a plutôt des bâtiments qui sont en bon état»* :

ou encore : *« on ne peut pas couvrir tous les chantiers en-même temps; la question se posera pour l'avenir à l'université de La Rochelle comme dans toutes les universités. Au niveau du patrimoine, je ne pense pas que cela soit un sujet si stratégique que cela pour l'université de La Rochelle et c'est surtout un sujet périlleux parce que financièrement ca engage sérieusement l'établissement et l'Etat. »*

Tableau 6.4

Formes	Khi2	Effectif Classe	%
*adm	50	45	26%
Bâtiment	45	7	100%
Emploi	43	18	57%
Patrimoine	38	8	78%
Poser	31	7	75%
Connaissance	30	5	100%
Echelle	30	5	100%
Couvrir	30	4	100%
Maintenir	30	4	100%
Instant	29	9	64%
Etat	28	15	46%
Sujet	24	6	71%
Année	24	13	42%
Choix	23	6	60%
établissement	23	13	37%
Question	23	14	39%
Deuxième	22	3	100%
Amortir	22	4	100%
Contrôler	22	4	80%
Prétention	22	3	100%
GVT	22	3	100%

Reste dans tous les cas l'inquiétude sur le point de savoir : *« est-ce-que l'Etat d'abord est capable de remettre à niveau l'établissement et puis [...] d'augmenter nos dotations pour que nous puissions couvrir, nous les annuités d'amortissement? »* Puisque : *« pour l'instant on n'est pas propriétaire donc on n'a pas à amortir nos bâtiments. [...] C'est quand-même une des-questions clé pour l'avenir »*. Au total, les marges de manœuvre, compte tenu de la contrainte financière, apparaissent réduites.

Le regroupement 3 : le discours du gouvernement

Il est tenu principalement par les élus dans les différents conseils pour représenter les courants de pensée (3.2.3.1.) mais aussi les composantes (3.2.3.2.).

Le sous-discours des instances

Le tableau 6.5 retrace les formes représentatives de la classe 4.

Tableau 6.5

Formes	Khi2	Effectif Classe	%
Conseil	217	77	74%
Scientifique	133	29	88%
Proposition	93	16	100%
Commission	58	11	91%
Administration	49	24	53%
Decision	47	15	61%
CA	40	13	65%
Finalement	37	13	61%
Siege	33	5	100%
*gouv	32	33	30%
Recherche	27	14	50%
Nomme	26	6	100%
CEVU	26	5	83%
Dossier	24	9	57%
Rôle	24	12	50%
CS	24	8	64%
Elu	21	6	71%
Mot	20	3	100%
Vide	20	3	100%
Instruction	20	5	100%

Ce discours tourne autour du rôle des instances, principalement du conseil (217) scientifique (137), mais aussi de celui des commissions (58) chargées de préparer en amont les propositions (93) pour des décisions (47) qui sont finalement prises en CA (40). Les phrases-types soulignent la répartition des rôles : « *ce n'est pas le président qui a le dernier mot, c'est le conseil d'administration. Alors concernant le CS et le CEVU, ceux sont des instances qui donnent des avis, qui proposent des choses, qui discutent sur des thèmes qui leur sont propres, donc la recherche pour le conseil scientifique* ».

Pour autant, cette répartition est contestée car les instances élues sont en partie dessaisies de leur pouvoir lors de la préparation des débats, ceux-ci étant largement discutés *ex ante* par des commissions composées de membres nommés : « *des groupes de travail qui sont en amont de ces conseils. En réalité, les conseils c'est plutôt des chambres d'enregistrement* ». Dans tous les cas : *« c'est quand-même lui [le président qui peut] contre l'avis du conseil d'administration, prendre la décision.* » C'est ce rôle prédominant du président qui se trouve dans le sous-discours suivant.

Le sous-discours du présidentialisme

Il est retranscrit dans le tableau n°6 constitué par le discours de la classe 5.

Tableau 6.6

Formes	Khi2	Effectif Classe	%
President	97	42	54%
Présidentiel	84	17	84%
Equipe	60	18	67%
Volonté	52	8	100%
Responsabilité	51	15	63%
Directeur	34	10	73%
Programme	26	4	100%
Associer	26	4	100%
Guillemet	25	5	83%
Consensus	25	5	83%
Réunion	19	5	80%
Piloter	19	4	80%
Présenter	19	3	100%
Tenir	19	3	100%
Ecrit	19	4	100%
UFR	19	5	80%
Bureau	17	5	63%
Autonomie	16	10	40%
Impact	15	4	67%
Passage	14	5	56%

Ce discours s'organise autour du président (97) et de l'équipe (60) présidentielle (84). Ainsi : « *le président actuel qui a voulu associer beaucoup plus d'étroitement les doyens et les directeurs de l'UFR à la gouvernance. En ce sens que depuis la domination des nouveaux présidents, les doyens et les directeurs de l'UFR font partie du bureau présidentiel.* » Ce présidentialisme est d'autant mieux accepté qu': *« au moment du passage à la RCE, il n'y a pas véritablement eu d'oppositions puisque ça faisait partie aussi du programme de campagne du président et de l'équipe présidentielle, il se présentait avec l'objectif prise de compétences élargies »*.

Discussion

La discussion des résultats s'organise autour de trois axes majeurs, à savoir en premier sur les espaces référentiels (3.2.4.1.), en second sur le présidentialisme (3.2.4.2.), sur la RCE (3.2.4.3.) et enfin sur l'état actuel de la gestion de l'université de la Rochelle (3.2.4.4.).

Sur les espaces référentiels

Il est rare, on l'a dit, d'aboutir à un rejet de 44% de l'analyse du corpus. A y regarder de près et à reprendre la lecture des verbatim, l'explication la plus plausible tient dans des séries de « petites » phrases incidentes et d'une tonalité générale émanant avant tout des administratifs de l'équipe présidentielle et du gouvernement de l'université expliquant chemin faisant, ou au détour d'un exposé que, de toutes façons, il n'y avait guère d'autres choix et qu'y aller rapidement permettait d'en retirer des avantages (effectivement 250 000 euros environ ont abondé le budget de l'ULR sur les deux premières années). Ces idées n'ont pas été longuement développées alors qu'elles ont certainement pesé dans l'engagement dans une sorte d'aventure LRU. Ce terme parait fondé en ce sens qu'une autre idée que l'on sent en filigrane, et qui ne ressort que par incidentes est celle du « challenge », du défi à relever qui donne une impression d'euphorie du type : cela nous sort d'une routine ; ou il va falloir trouver (inventer) des solutions, bref, par l'imprégnation d'un langage managérial et par la glorification de ces difficultés.

Sur le présidentialisme

À ce sujet, la LRU est appliquée dans toutes ses dimensions et c'est bien le président, qui, *in fine,* prend les décisions conformément à son programme électoral. Il prend soin cependant de consulter les différents conseils, dont le rôle, à l'exception du CA apparait affaibli du fait de la préparation des débats par des experts nommés, prenant le risque d'aboutir à une contestation, du fait que ces conseils peuvent ne plus apparaître que comme (sic) *« des chambres d'enregistrement »* avec parfois des difficultés pour obtenir les *quorums.* Jusqu'ici toutefois cette gêne ne s'est révélée que marginale et a laissé au président le champ libre pour appliquer son programme.

Sur la RCE

C'est là que le bât blesse et que la contestation est la plus virulente, de la part des syndicats, mais globalement du personnel, sur la question des primes (et du régime indemnitaire), des modulations de service et de l'attribution des postes. Le gel de ces derniers par le gouvernement rend la marge de manœuvre d'autant plus réduite que le nombre d'étudiants est en augmentation, rendant l'encadrement de ces derniers plus délicat dans certaines filières (la gestion en particulier) avec la tentation de réduire le contenu des maquettes.

Les solutions ne sont guère simples pour pallier le manque de dotations financières, la création d'une fondation pouvant éventuellement aider l'ULR sur ce point. La possibilité de se servir du patrimoine immobilier pour gérer la pénurie semble écartée, et la crainte de personnels reste bien celle de l'abandon, au moins partiel, de la notion de service public.

L'université malade de la gestion ?

Au total, il est difficile de percevoir un *bonus* net du passage à la LRU et aux RCE. La démocratie n'y a pas gagné du fait de l'affaiblissement du rôle des conseils et surtout de la présence affirmée d'experts nommés. Derrière une euphorie de façade marquée par les dirigeants, on sent rapidement se dessiner un doute sur l'avenir de l'Université de La Rochelle Quel sera son rôle ? De proximité, dotée de faibles moyens, luttant pour conserver les M et D ? Pour paraphraser le titre de l'ouvrage de De Gaulejac (2005) : la société malade de la gestion, on peut s'interroger si le service public doit, et à quel prix, s'installer dans une logique gestionnaire. L'université ne serait-elle pas malade de la gestion ?

Comme l'expose De Gaulejac, sous une apparence pragmatique, la gestion constitue une idéologie qui légitime la guerre économique, l'obsession du rendement financier. La culture de la performance et de la compétition met tout le monde sous haute pression : épuisement professionnel, stress. L'université sera-t-elle condamnée à gérer aussi, comme Orange, des suicides au travail. Cette culture du rendement sacralisé par les différents classements : Shangaï pour les universités, AERES, pour les universitaires, à un point tel qu'en dépend leur carrière sur des critères éminemment contestables (Charreaux et Gervais, 2007), l'université n'est plus un espace de création de la connaissance, mais un simple marché, un champ de bataille où le remède proposé consiste toujours à durcir la lutte.

La gouvernance des universités, également contaminée par le « réalisme gestionnaire », semble impuissante à dessiner une autre voie. L'université ne serait-elle condamnée à n'être plus qu'un instrument supplémentaire de la « servitude libérale » comme l'exprime Beauvois (1994) dans son analyse de la soumission ? Peut-on échapper à l'épidémie? Le service public d'enseignement supérieur est-il soluble dans une vision managériale de l'université ? Cette question reste entière et c'est bien à cette réflexion que contribue cet article.

Conclusion

La LRU s'est installée dans l'ULR avec la RCE. À partir de neuf entretiens approfondis avec les principaux dirigeants politiques et administratifs de l'université et des syndicats, et une exploitation des données menée avec le logiciel ALCESTE 2010, trois discours types sont repérés : sur le service public ; sur les marges de manœuvre ; sur le gouvernement de l'université. À la question de recherche sur le point de savoir quel bonus ou quel malus l'ULR avait retiré de cette autonomie et de l'installation dans une logique gestionnaire, il semble que l'on aboutisse à une sorte de compensation, mais que des doutes subsistent sur l'avenir de cette université qui va devoir s'interroger sur la gestion de ses personnels, et sur la gestion de celui-ci. La phase d'euphorie liée à la création semble passée et la contestation des personnels, en particulier les IATOS sur la mobilité interne amène récemment un préavis de grève pour la venue de l'AERES et un recul de la présidence sur ce point de la mobilité laisse à penser que les difficultés sont à venir. Concernant le paradigme de gouvernance et son appréhension dans une université de service public, ce dernier diffère de tout sens lorsqu'on tient compte du contexte de la gouvernance dans une entreprise managériale. Dans le système universitaire, les résultats font apparaître que le « gouvernement » prône sur le concept de « gouvernance » étant donné que les grandes orientations stratégiques de l'université demeurent dépendantes des décisions du président de l'université. Le rôle du conseil d'administration, en termes du contrôle de décisions de l'exécutif, apparaît comme un organe d'assistance du président, plutôt qu'un organe de contrôle auquel revient l'approbation de l'exécution des grandes décisions stratégiques.

Bibliographie

Andès (Association française des docteurs) (2009), « Autonomie des universités versus autonomie des universitaires ? Quelle gouvernance est possible et souhaitable ? », Matinée du samedi 12 mai 2007, Institut Henri Poincaré, Paris. 11pages.

Alix-Desfautaux C. (1998), « Triangulation : vers un dépassement de l'opposition qualitatif / quantitatif », *Économies et Sociétés, série SG*, n° 2, 1998, p 209-223.

Barthelemy F., Beraud A. et Martin M., (2009), « La loi LRU a-t-elle modifie les distributions de pouvoir au sein des universités françaises ? », Revue économique, 2009/6 (Vol. 60).

Barthelemy M. (2009), « Compte rendu du 8ème Grand Débat de l'EHESS, « Refonder l'Université », 20/05/09 », *Revue du MAUSS permanente*, 11 juin 2009, [en ligne]. http://www.journaldumauss.net/spip.php?article522

Caby J., Hirigoyen G. (2001), « la création de valeur de l'entreprise », *Economica*, 2001 (2ème édition).

Chamberlain, D., Gordon, G. et Plunkett, L. (1993), « Improving accountability in colleges and universities», Internal Auditing, Spring 1993.

Charles, C. et Verger, J., (2007), « Histoire des universités », *Paris: Presses universitaires de France*, 2007, p 5, *in* Gras I. (2010), *« la loi LRU et les bibliothèques universitaires »*, Mémoire d'étude - Janvier 2010, sous la direction de François Cavalier, école nationale supérieure des sciences de l'information et des bibliothèques, E.N.N.S.I.B., 112 pages.

Charreaux G. (1997), « "Introduction générale" et "Vers une théorie du gouvernement d'entreprise" », *in* Charreaux G. (éd.) « Le gouvernement des entreprises : Corporate Governance, théories et faits », *Economica*, pp. 1-13 et pp. 421–469.

Charreaux, G. et Gervais, M. (2007), « La piste aux étoiles, Finance Contrôle Stratégie » – Préface, volume 10, n° 4, décembre 2007, p. 5 - 16.

Cohen E., (2009), « La réforme de la gouvernance des universités », *séance du lundi 6 juillet 2009,* site de l'ASMP, http://www.asmp.fr/travaux/communications/2009/cohen.htm

De Gaulejac, V., (2005), « La société malade de la gestion ; idéologie gestionnaire, pouvoir managérial et harcèlement social », Seuil

CQSU/AFPC/FTQ (2009), « Mémoire du Conseil québécois des syndicats universitaires de l'AFPC au Québec concernant les projets de loi 38 et 44 sur la gouvernance des institutions d'enseignement post-secondaire québécoises ». Mémoire déposé à la Commission de l'éducation de l'Assemblée nationale du Québec le 17 août 2009. http://sesum.org/pdf/MemoireGouvernanceCQSU-aout09.pdf

Fama, E.F. et Jensen, M.C. (1983), "Separation of Ownership and Control", *Journal of Law and Economics,* Vol. 26, n° 2, (June 1983), pp. 301–325.

Finance J.P. (2007), « Gouvernance et autonomie des universités et conséquences sur le système français de recherche et d'innovation »,

Colloque FutuRIS *du 21 juin 2007,* Quelles perspectives pour un système français de recherche et d'innovation en mutation ?, 7 pages.

Jensen, M.C. et Meckling, W.H. (1976), "Theory of the firm: managerial behavior, agency costs and ownership structure", *Journal of financial economics,* (Octobre 1976), pp.305-360.

Laurent D. (2006), « Enseignement supérieur : aborder la compétition mondiale à armes égales ? », *Gouvernance des universités : la condition préalable à l'autonomie*, Tribunes web.

Machina H., (2009), « La LRU, ses conséquences en termes de gouvernance, et le mouvement universitaire en France », [consultable en ligne].http://www.fqppu.org/assets/files/bibliotheque/bulletin/juin_2009/communication_gouvernance_machinal.pdf

Marc E., (1994), « Quelles démarches en psychologie? », *Sciences Humaines*, n°35, Janvier, p 19-22.

Paillé P, et Mucchielli A., (2003), « L'analyse qualitative en Sciences Humaines et Sociales », Paris, Armand Colin, 2003, 211 pages.

Schaub J-F (2009), « Loi LRU : pour une clarification des situations dans l'Université », http://www.rue89.com

Wacheux F. (1996), « Méthodes qualitatives et recherche en gestion », Paris, Economica, 1996, 281 p.

Annexe 1 : Liste des établissements accédant aux RCE au 1er janvier 2009

Cette sélection concerne 312 000 étudiants, soit 22% de l'effectif total.

Nom	Effectif
Aix-Marseille-II (Méditerranée)	21 000
Cergy-Pontoise	12 600
Clermont-Ferrand-I (Auvergne)	13 300
Corte	4 000
Limoges	14 300
Lyon-I Claude-Bernard	29 500
Marne-la-Vallée	10 500
Montpellier-I	20 500
Mulhouse Haute-Alsace	7 500
Nancy-I Henri-Poincaré	12 500
Paris-Descartes (Paris-V)	31 100
UPMC (Paris-VI)	29 400
Paris-Diderot (Paris-VII)	24 700
La Rochelle	6 500
Saint-Étienne Jean-Monnet	14 000
Strasbourg-I Louis-Pasteur	18 800
Strasbourg-II Marc-Bloch	11 900
Strasbourg-III Robert-Schuman	9 900
Toulouse-I Sciences sociales	16 600
UTT (université technologique de Troyes)	3 500

Annexe 2 : Guide d'entretien

Ouverture

1. Comment définiriez-vous la Loi L.R.U. ? Quelles sont ses objectifs ?

2. Quelles sont les problématiques auxquelles la loi L.R.U permet de répondre et auxquelles le système de gouvernance précédent n'y parvenait pas ?

Approfondissement

3. Quels sont les axes stratégiques autour desquels l'université devrait se centrer afin de répondre aux finalités attendues par la L.R.U. ?

4. Pourriez-vous nous décrire le processus de prise de décisions ? Qui prend la décision au niveau des grandes orientations stratégiques ? Comment s'effectue la mise en œuvre d'une véritable politique d'établissement ?

5. En termes de compétences et connaissances, comment la « gouvernance élargie » est incorporée dans la vision stratégique de l'université ? Autrement dit, comment la logique de recrutement et de sélection des candidats est-elle perçue en vue de valoriser le capital humain dans l'établissement académique ainsi que la qualité d'enseignement ?

6. Dans l'ensemble, les décisions majeures reviennent au Président de l'université. Selon vous, comment l'équilibre peut être maintenu entre les consultations émanant des divers conseils (C.S, C.E.V.U. et C.A.) et les décisions centralisées ?

7. Dans quelle optique la démocratie universitaire peut-elle être élaborée ? Cela dit, le Président de l'université peut décider de tout alors qu'une forme de minimisation des rôles est constatée. S'agit-il dans ce cas d'une véritable répartition des pouvoirs ?

8. D'après vous, quelles sont les perspectives professionnelles et culturelles par rapport auxquelles la loi L.R.U. positionne l'université ?

Conclusion

9. Quelle valeur ajoutée que pourrait la L.R.U. apporter par rapport à l'ancien système de gouvernance ?

10. Votre opinion sur le futur des universités en France suite à la loi LRU.

L'IMPACT DES MECANISMES DE GOUVERNANCE SUR LA DIVULGATION D'INFORMATIONS DES ENTREPRISES FRANÇAISES

AYMEN AJINA

Résumé

Le présent article a pour objectif d'étudier les facteurs relatifs aux mécanismes de gouvernance d'entreprise qui déterminent l'étendue de la divulgation d'informations des entreprises françaises. Notre échantillon regroupe 155 entreprises françaises, sur une période s'étalant de 2008 à 2009. Les résultats montrent que la taille du conseil d'administration, l'ancienneté moyenne des membres, le nombre des réunions, et le cumul des rôles de chef de direction et du président du conseil contribuent à l'amélioration de l'étendue de la divulgation d'informations. Ces résultats nous mènent à recommander aux entreprises françaises de bien jouer sur ces variables pour renforcer leurs mécanismes d'informations. En effet, la transparence du marché français doit passer par la mise en place de plus de contraintes sur ce système. Ces contraintes sont liées spécifiquement aux caractéristiques du conseil d'administration.

Mots clés : Gouvernement d'entreprise, conseil d'administration, divulgation d'informations.

Abstract

This article aims to examine the factors related to corporate governance mechanisms that determine the extent of information disclosure related to French companies. Our sample includes 155 companies French, for a period ranging from 2008 to 2009. The results show that the size of the board, the average age of members, the number of meetings, and the multiple roles of CEO and Chairman of the Board contribute to the improvement of the extent of information disclosure.

These results recommend that French companies to play on these variables to improve their information mechanisms. Indeed, the transparency of the French market has to go through the establishment of more constraints on this system. These constraints are specifically related to the characteristics of the board of directors.
Keywords: Corporate governance, board of directors, disclosure of information.

Introduction

La transparence informationnelle est l'une des conditions nécessaires à l'efficience des marchés. Ceci explique que les autorités boursières exigent aux entreprises émettrices qu'elles publient, en temps et en heure, une information complète et précise. Néanmoins, cette exigence se heurte à la volonté des dirigeants d'entreprises de maintenir confidentielles certaines informations stratégiques. Cette possibilité, donnée aux dirigeants d'entreprise, de conserver par devers eux des informations privilégiées sous certaines conditions, introduit une moindre divulgation d'informations sur le marché. Etant donné la marge dont disposent les dirigeants dans la divulgation d'informations, les actionnaires disposent d'une variété de mécanismes pour protéger leurs intérêts (Jensen et Meckling, 1976). Ces mécanismes comprennent les variables relatives au gouvernement d'entreprise.

Charreaux définit le gouvernement d'entreprise comme :

> « *L'ensemble des mécanismes organisationnels qui ont pour effet de délimiter les pouvoirs et d'influencer les décisions des dirigeants, autrement dit, qui « gouvernent » leur conduite et définissent leur espace discrétionnaire* ».

A travers ses rôles, notamment de contrôle et d'évaluation des compétences des dirigeants, de suivi de la performance des entreprises et de vérification de la bonne exécution des engagements de ces dernières avec ses différents partenaires, la divulgation d'informations est considérée comme l'enjeu et l'une des priorités que le système de gouvernance des entreprises doit garantir.

Ce concept puise son origine dans les développements de la théorie de l'agence (Jensen et Meckling, 1976). Néanmoins, le cadre d'analyse de l'association entre mécanismes de gouvernement d'entreprise et divulgation d'informations est la résultante d'autres hypothèses théoriques, telles que la théorie de l'enracinement, la théorie de l'intendance et la théorie de la dépendance (Shleifer et Vishny, 1989 ; Donaldson, 1990).

L'interrogation sur les déterminants de la divulgation d'informations a fait le débat de plusieurs recherches[1]. Toutefois, ces études ne font pas référence à la manière dont les entreprises sont gouvernées. Ils sont très rares les travaux qui ont essayé d'intégrer, dans le cadre d'une même approche, une panoplie de facteurs susceptibles d'évaluer le mode de gouvernance des firmes afin d'expliquer la politique informationnelle. D'autant plus que ce thème de recherche a suscité peu d'intérêt dans le domaine académique (Xie et al, 2002 ; Chtourou, Bédard et Courteau, 2001; Klein, 2002) par rapport aux multiples essaies des organismes des tutelles (Blue Ribbon Committee aux États-Unis, Viénot I et II, Bouton, et le Code MEDEF-AFEP en France). Cet article fournit de nouvelles preuves empiriques et apporte certaines contributions par rapport à cette littérature antérieure. En effet, l'étude s'intéresse à un aspect bien particulier de la performance à savoir: la transparence de l'entreprise.

Le cas français nous a paru un terrain d'investigation intéressant en raison de son environnement de gouvernement d'entreprise et de l'émergence de nouvelles pratiques comptables ajustées par rapport aux normes internationales. En effet, notre période d'étude est marquée par l'application des normes IFRS[2]. Ces normes ont pour objectif d'harmoniser certaines informations financières des entreprises, de préserver la confiance envers les marchés financiers et de faciliter les négociations.

Les résultats de l'étude montrent que la taille du conseil d'administration, l'ancienneté moyenne des membres, le nombre des réunions, et le cumul des rôles de chef de direction et du président du conseil contribuent à l'amélioration de l'étendue de la divulgation d'informations. Cet article est organisé comme suit : la première section illustre la littérature reliant l'étendue de la divulgation d'informations aux mécanismes de gouvernance d'entreprise. La deuxième section présente l'échantillon et la méthodologie utilisée, suivis des résultats et discussions. La dernière section conclut l'étude.

---

[1] Paturel et al. (2006) au Royaume-Uni et en France; Lakhal (2005) en France; Xiao et al. (2004) en Chine; Marston et Polei (2004) en Allemagne; Ettredge et al (2002) aux Etats-Unis.

[2] IFRS: International Financial Reporting Standards.

1. Mécanismes de gouvernance d'entreprise et divulgation d'informations

Conseil d'administration et divulgation d'informations

Le rapport Bouton (2002) définit le rôle du conseil d'administration comme suit :

> *« Le conseil d'administration détermine les orientations de l'activité de la société et veille à leur mise en œuvre. Sous réserve des pouvoirs expressément attribués aux assemblées d'actionnaires et dans la limite de l'objet social, il se saisit de toute question intéressant la bonne marche de la société et règle par ses délibérations les affaires qui la concernent ».*

Attig et Morck (2005) trouvent que si le conseil fonctionne efficacement, le niveau d'asymétrie d'informations devrait être faible. Par ailleurs, le conseil d'administration est une structure complexe qui doit répondre à certaines caractéristiques de taille, d'indépendance et de structure administrative afin d'accomplir son rôle de contrôle avec efficacité.

La taille du conseil : Les hypothèses de la théorie d'agence stipulent que la taille élevée du conseil d'administration favorise la domination du dirigeant en faisant naître des coalitions et des conflits de groupe (Jensen, 1993). Il en résulte des conseils fragmentés ayant du mal à fonctionner efficacement et éprouvant des difficultés à trouver un consensus sur les décisions. Ainsi, la manipulation des évaluations des administrateurs en est largement facilitée, ce qui a pour conséquence une moindre information publiée. Ginglinger (2002) suggère que la présence de nombreux administrateurs dans le conseil amplifie les conflits entre eux et accroît l'existence de passagers clandestins. Abbott et *al.* (2004), dans le contexte anglo-saxon, suggèrent l'existence d'une relation négative entre la taille du conseil d'administration et le contenu informatif du résultat.

Cependant, selon la théorie de la dépendance envers les ressources, l'amélioration des relations des entreprises avec les différentes parties prenantes est devenue possible dans le cadre de conseils élargis. Cela permet un accès facilité à l'expertise et une meilleure communication avec l'environnement. Agrawal et Knoeber (1999) confirment cette hypothèse et trouvent que le conseil de taille élevée est plus adapté pour les entreprises où les informations sont difficiles à obtenir. Chtourou, Bédard et Courteau (2001) ont démontré qu'un conseil d'administration de grande taille aide à contrôler la discrétion des dirigeants. Cet effet favorable sur le contrôle des dirigeants entraîne une influence positive sur la politique informationnelle de l'entreprise.

Anderson et *al.* (2004) soutiennent cet argument et affirment que la taille élevée du conseil fournit une supervision supérieure du procédé de la comptabilité financière, donc l'entreprise offre ainsi une meilleure transparence. Par ailleurs, Jeanjean (2002) et Firth et *al.* (2007) ne trouvent aucun lien significatif entre la taille du CA et la transparence de l'entreprise dans le contexte français et chinois respectivement. La variable (adm_taille) représente le nombre d'administrateurs dans le conseil d'administration de chaque entreprise de l'échantillon.

Hypothèse$_1$: La taille du conseil d'administration a un impact sur l'étendue de la divulgation d'informations.

L'indépendance des administrateurs : selon la théorie de l'agence, les administrateurs internes ne disposent pas du pouvoir suffisant pour contester les choix des dirigeants. Ces administrateurs sont des cadres de l'entreprise ou des salariés qui dépendent hiérarchiquement des personnes qu'ils doivent contrôler. Il est par conséquent difficile de s'opposer à leurs responsables hiérarchiques directs. Au contraire, les administrateurs indépendants pèsent plus favorablement sur les décisions des dirigeants. Ces derniers seraient ainsi plus contraints à informer régulièrement le marché (Dahya et *al.*, 2008). Relaxant l'hypothèse de la théorie de l'agence, Patelli et Prencipe (2007) mettent en évidence une relation positive et significative entre l'indépendance du conseil d'administration et la diffusion volontaire d'informations pour les entreprises italiennes. Similairement, la théorie de la dépendance envers les ressources stipule que l'entreprise doit nommer des administrateurs externes afin de contrôler l'incertitude de l'environnement informationnel et d'assurer sa pérennité.

Beasley (1996) conclut sur un échantillon de 75 entreprises américaines durant la période 1980-1991 que la présence de ces administrateurs améliore l'efficacité de contrôle du management et elle prévient les fraudes comptables. En examinant l'association entre les administrateurs externes et l'étendue de l'information dans les divulgations financières obligatoires à Hong kong, Chen et Jaggi (2000) ont trouvé un lien positif. Ce résultat est expliqué par le fait que la présence des administrateurs indépendants dans le conseil d'administration renforce la conformité de l'entreprise aux exigences réglementaires. Plus récemment, Cornett et al. (2006) valident l'hypothèse selon laquelle les accruals discrétionnaires sont négativement liés à l'efficacité du conseil d'administration, mesurée par la proportion d'administrateurs externes.

Au contraire, la théorie de l'enracinement prédit que les administrateurs externes n'ont pas le pouvoir suffisant pour s'opposer aux stratégies mises en œuvre par les dirigeants pour accroître leur pouvoir sur les partenaires. Eng et Mak (2003) ont trouvé qu'un accroissement de la proportion des administrateurs externes réduisait la divulgation d'informations volontaires par les dirigeants de l'entreprise. Ce résultat, bien qu'il soit en contradiction avec ceux de Chen et Jaggi (2000) et Forker (1992), est consistant avec une relation de substitution entre les administrateurs externes et la divulgation dans le contrôle des dirigeants. En effet, une présence accrue de membres externes accroit l'indépendance du conseil ; ainsi ses membres sont alors plus aptes à obtenir de l'information pour contrôler les dirigeants. Gul et Leung (2004) soutiennent cette hypothèse. Ils montrent une association négative entre la proportion des administrateurs externes et l'étendue de divulgation d'informations pour les entreprises cotées à Hong Kong.

Par ailleurs, Ho et Wong (2001), en utilisant des données de Hong Kong, montrent que la présence des administrateurs indépendants n'affecte pas l'étendue des informations publiées. Ce résultat ne corrobore pas le résultat de Chen et Jaggi (2000). En effet, Ho et Wong (2001) expliquent que la présence des indépendants assure seulement la conformité de l'entreprise aux exigences réglementaires de divulgation et n'influence pas l'étendue de la divulgation d'informations.

Enfin, Fama et Jensen (1983) affirment qu'un conseil d'administration a besoin d'autant d'administrateurs externes que d'administrateurs internes pour accomplir les tâches qui lui incombent. Il semble ainsi que l'efficacité du conseil d'administration résulte d'un compromis entre l'indépendance et l'expertise des administrateurs internes.

Pour apprécier l'indépendance des administrateurs, nous avons adopté les recommandations du Code AFEP-MEDEF (2008). Ainsi un administrateur est considéré comme indépendant lorsqu'il ne maintient aucune relation avec l'entreprise ou sa direction qui puisse compromettre l'exercice de sa liberté de jugement (Annexe).

H_2 : La présence d'administrateurs indépendants au sein du conseil d'administration a un impact positif sur la divulgation d'informations.

L'expertise financière des administrateurs (adm_exp) : plusieurs débats sur la gouvernance des entreprises tournent autour de la composition des conseils d'administration. Quant à l'intéressement au niveau de compétence financière des administrateurs, Güner et al. (2008)

trouvent que l'existence des administrateurs experts dans le contrôle financier pourrait affecter les politiques de divulgations des entreprises à travers une information complète et plus précise. Dans ce sens, Wagner (2008) ajoute que lors de la composition d'un conseil d'administration, un compromis entre indépendance et compétence doit exister pour une meilleure efficacité du groupe.

Ce n'est qu'avec la publication du rapport Bouton (2002) qu'on a commencé à parler de la compétence des administrateurs dans le contrôle des états financiers. Le but de l'intégration de cette variable cible à déceler l'aptitude des administrateurs dans la compréhension et le contrôle des mécanismes d'informations. Les entreprises sont incitées ainsi, par ce rapport, à nommer des administrateurs compétents tout en restant silencieux sur la définition de cette compétence. C'est pour cette raison, nous nous sommes référé à la démarche de Jeanjean et Stolowy (2009), Wagner (2008) et du rapport du *Blue Ribbon Committee* (1999) pour définir l'expertise. Ainsi, nous avons désigné comme expert financier tout administrateur qui répond aux critères suivants :

- L'expertise est assignée en fonction de la formation académique(1) et/ou de la carrière (2) de l'administrateur.

(1) : nous assignons l'expertise financière à tout administrateur diplômé d'une école de commerce ou d'une université dans le domaine de la gestion, touchant la comptabilité ou la finance.

(2) : nous assignons l'expertise financière à tout administrateur qui a exercé ou qui exerce des fonctions à vocation financière. Sont considérés ainsi experts financiers les directeurs financiers, inspecteurs financiers, les auditeurs et les juristes des cours des comptes, ainsi que toute autre fonction assimilée.

Selon la qualification de l'expertise, une variable binaire prend la valeur 1 lorsque l'administrateur est expert financier, 0 sinon.

H_3 : l'expertise financière des administrateurs améliore la divulgation d'informations.

Ancienneté des administrateurs (adm_anc) : La durée du service dans un conseil d'administration est un indicateur de familiarisation avec l'activité de l'entreprise. Tandis que la familiarisation peut aider un administrateur à exercer ses droits de surveillance, elle peut aussi être un indicateur d'enracinement et d'inefficacité (Koppes et *al.*, 1999). Beasley (1996) prétend que l'ancienneté renforce la capacité des administrateurs à exercer un contrôle sur la haute direction. Plus les administrateurs sont expérimentés plus leur mandat est assuré au sein de l'entreprise, et plus ils sont en mesure de résister aux pressions de groupes allant dans le sens des souhaits de la direction. Beasley (1996) trouve une relation négative entre le nombre moyen d'années pendant lesquelles les administrateurs ont siégé au conseil d'administration et la probabilité d'émettre des états financiers frauduleux, suggérant ainsi que l'ancienneté augmente la capacité des administrateurs à surveiller efficacement la direction et la divulgation d'informations de l'entreprise. Ce résultat confirme l'hypothèse de la théorie de l'intendance. Cependant, la familiarisation avec l'activité d'une entreprise peut conduire à l'incapacité des administrateurs à reconnaître les problèmes potentiels et à retenir un regard objectif sur l'entreprise résultant d'un excès de confiance. La variable (adm_anc) mesure l'ancienneté moyenne des membres du conseil d'administration d'une entreprise donnée à une année t.

H4 : L'ancienneté des administrateurs affecte la divulgation d'informations

La périodicité et l'assiduité des membres du conseil d'administration aux réunions : un conseil d'administration plus actif est sensé effectuer plus de réunions qu'un conseil d'administration inefficace. Menon et Williams (1994) et Uzun et al. (2004) suggèrent que cette variable peut fournir une idée sur les conseils d'administration actives et ceux de figuration. Pour garantir une efficacité et bonne communication de la part de l'équipe dirigeante, le conseil d'administration doit veiller à une certaine périodicité des réunions des administrateurs.

Le rapport Viénot avance que les conseils doivent se réunir lorsque les circonstances l'exigent et, à défaut de circonstances particulières, quatre à six réunions par an sont suffisantes pour contrôler la marche du groupe et prendre des décisions essentielles. En outre, le conseil d'administration doit permettre un examen et une discussion approfondis des matières relevant de la compétence du conseil et des attributions dévolues aux comités du conseil. Godard et Schatt (2004) décrivent les principales caractéristiques de 97 conseils d'administration français en 2002 et leur fonctionnement. Ils constatent que le nombre moyen des réunions est de l'ordre de 7 fois par an (la médiane est égale à 6), soit environ tous les deux mois. Les résultats de l'étude menée par ces derniers témoignent également de fortes disparités entre les entreprises[3]. Jenkins (2002) montre

---

[3] Les auteurs constatent que moins de 15% des conseils se réunissent désormais au maximum quatre fois par an.

qu'une plus grande fréquence de rencontres du comité contribue à une meilleure qualité de l'information financière.

L'assiduité des membres du conseil d'administration aux réunions de ce dernier peut également être un facteur déterminant de la qualité des travaux de ce dernier notamment en matière de contrôle de la divulgation d'informations. L'étude de Godard et Schatt (2004) montre un taux d'assiduité égal à 84% (pour les 66 entreprises qui ont fourni des indications sur la présence des membres lors des réunions). Si l'assiduité est à peu près la même, il apparaît que le nombre de réunions a augmenté significativement en 20 ans. La variable (adm_reu) mesure le nombre des réunions effectuées durant une année

H_5: le nombre des réunions du conseil d'administration a un impact positif sur la divulgation d'informations.

La structure moniste dans le conseil : les entreprises dans lesquelles une même personne cumule les fonctions de directeur général et de président du conseil d'administration sont considérées comme ayant des structures monistes dans le conseil. L'analyse de la relation entre la divulgation d'informations et le cumul des fonctions de direction et de contrôle, dévoile des constats théoriques et empiriques mitigés. Suite aux recommandations du rapport Viénot (1999), inspirées du modèle anglo-saxon, les fonctions de président de conseil d'administration et de directeur général peuvent être dissociées. Ensuite, la loi du 15 mai 2001 relative aux nouvelles régulations économiques (NRE) vient créer un nouveau mode d'organisation de la société anonyme dans lequel les fonctions de président du conseil d'administration et de directeur général sont dissociées.

Selon la théorie de l'agence (Jensen et Meckling, 1976 ; Fama et Jensen, 1983), la concentration du pouvoir, résultant de la dualité des postes de chef de la direction et de président du conseil, signale l'absence de séparation des décisions de gestion et de celles de contrôle. Par contre, la dissociation des deux fonctions devrait assurer un meilleur équilibre des pouvoirs entre d'une part le conseil d'administration chargé de contrôle de la gestion, et d'autre part le directeur général, véritable chef d'entreprise qui serait davantage placé en position de subordination par rapport aux représentants des actionnaires. De ce qui précède on peut supposer qu'il serait plus vraisemblable que les entreprises avec une dualité de postes de chef de la direction et de président du conseil soient associées à des niveaux plus bas de divulgation d'informations, puisque le conseil serait moins efficace dans le contrôle des dirigeants et dans l'assurance d'un plus haut niveau de transparence. Cette supposition a été confirmée empiriquement par l'étude de Forker (1992).

Néanmoins, la théorie de l'intendance et la théorie de la dépendance envers les ressources affirment que la concentration du pouvoir du PDG est bénéfique pour l'entreprise et elle facilite la prise de décision et l'acquisition des ressources nécessaires à l'entreprise. Haniffa et Cooke (2002) trouvent une association négative entre la concentration du pouvoir et la divulgation d'informations pour les entreprises Malaisiennes. Ces résultats infirment l'hypothèse suggérant qu'un président externe renforce l'indépendance du conseil d'administration. Ils concluent ainsi, que le président externe du conseil a une grande utilité pour détenir les informations privées. Par ailleurs, Ho et Wong (2001) montrent que le cumul des fonctions n'influence pas l'étendue de la diffusion d'informations. Ils expliquent ce résultat par le fait que la personne qui occupe les postes du directeur général et du président du conseil d'administration, est généralement un actionnaire important de l'entreprise. Selon l'existence ou pas d'une dualité de fonction, la variable (adm_dua) est définie comme une variable muette égale à 1 en cas de structure moniste dans le conseil, et 0 sinon.

H_6 : Il existe une relation négative entre la présence d'une structure moniste et l'étendue de la divulgation d'informations.

Les caractéristiques des entreprises

Taille de l'entreprise : La théorie de l'agence suggère que les entreprises de grande taille ont des coûts d'agence relativement plus élevés que les petites entreprises. La taille de l'entreprise est souvent le facteur le plus déterminant de l'étendue de la divulgation d'informations (Meek et al. 1995 ; Labelle, 2002). Ainsi, les entreprises de grande taille disposent des ressources plus importantes pour avoir une politique plus clair des mécanismes d'informations et les coûts qu'elles encourent sont moindres en raison des économies d'échelle. Relaxant l'hypothèse de la théorie des coûts d'informations, Lang et Lundholm (1993) montrent que les entreprises de grande taille adoptent une politique de divulgation plus prononcée que celles de petite taille parce qu'une telle politique leur procure de nombreux avantages en termes nets. Elle leur permet, grâce aux économies d'échelles, de légitimer leurs décisions aux différents partenaires (créanciers, investisseurs, employés etc.) à un coût inférieur à celui supporté par les petites entreprises. Selon Arbel *et al.* (1983), Collins *et al.* (1987), Freeman (1987) et Shores (1990), les informations qui concernent les grandes entreprises intéressant généralement un plus grand nombre d'investisseurs que celles relatives aux entreprises de plus petite taille. En effet, les analystes financiers suivent tout particulièrement ces grandes entreprises, ce qui améliore leur visibilité. Eng et Mak (2003) montre l'existence d'une relation positive entre la taille de l'entreprise et l'étendue de l'information présentée par les entreprises cotées à la Bourse de Toronto au sujet de leurs pratiques de gouvernance.

La performance : Les modèles de signal offrent un terrain riche et intéressant pour analyser l'offre d'informations. S'appuyant sur l'hypothèse de la théorie de signal, Verrechia (1983) a démontré qu'en présence des coûts d'informations, seules les informations favorables sont diffusées pour accroître la valeur de l'entreprise. En effet, si l'entreprise veut attirer et fidéliser les investisseurs afin de réduire son coût du capital, elle sera incitée à signaler sa performance. Au contraire, les dirigeants qui sont dotés de faibles performances peuvent se sentir menacés et sont susceptibles de dissimuler de faibles résultats enregistrés (Miller et Piotroski, 2000). Par conséquent, Penman (1980) montre que les entreprises aux mauvaises perspectives évitent de communiquer alors que celles aux bonnes perspectives publient plus d'informations. Mauldin et Richtermeyer (2004) ont montré que le niveau de la divulgation dans les rapports annuels augmente avec l'importance de la performance comptable. Ce résultat souligne que les dirigeants sont incités à divulguer l'information, surtout lorsque la valeur de l'entreprise augmente. Toutefois, d'autres études empiriques ne valident pas l'hypothèse de la performance (Ettredge et *al.*, 2002). En examinant les mécanismes d'informations des grandes entreprises françaises cotées, Bertrand (2000) a trouvé que la réalisation de moindres performances pousse les entreprises à améliorer leur divulgation. Ce résultat s'explique par le souci des entreprises de préserver leur réputation et d'éviter les conséquences négatives (risque de contentieux) qu'elles encourent si elles n'alertent pas le marché en cas de faible performance.

L'endettement : Dans le cadre de la théorie de l'agence, Jensen et Meckling (1976) ont montré que les coûts d'agence liés aux conflits d'intérêt entre actionnaires et créanciers augmentent avec le niveau d'endettement de l'entreprise. Les créanciers demandent aux dirigeants des informations sur la firme pour s'assurer de la capacité de l'entreprise à rembourser sa dette à l'échéance. La diffusion d'informations volontaires est ainsi importante pour réduire ces coûts d'agence de la dette qui naissent des divergences d'intérêt entre les actionnaires et les créanciers, en vue d'attirer et donner confiance aux créanciers (Andrikopoulos et al., 2007). Ainsi, un endettement élevé est théoriquement synonyme à des pratiques favorables au gouvernement d'entreprise et à la divulgation d'informations. Selon Debreceny et al. (2002), afin d'assurer ses créanciers de sa capacité à rembourser, l'entreprise endettée aurait tendance à diffuser plus d'informations. Dès lors, le ratio dettes long terme sur le total de l'actif serait lié positivement à la stratégie de divulgation d'informations.

Cependant, en se référant à l'hypothèse de la théorie de *free cash flows*, Jensen (1986) soulève que l'endettement est un moyen efficace pour réduire efficacement les coûts d'agence. Cet auteur suggère qu'un fort endettement permet d'éviter le comportement opportuniste des dirigeants et de contrôler le problème de *free cash flows*, tout en réduisant les bénéfices privés restant à la disposition des managers et afin d'éviter l'investissement dans des projets à faible performance. L'endettement est ainsi considéré comme un substitut au renforcement de la divulgation d'informations.

Le secteur d'activité : Les résultats des études empiriques sur la relation entre le secteur d'activité et l'étendue de la divulgation d'informations sont mitigés. Haven *et al.* (2002) et Kasznik et Lev (1995) ont montré l'existence d'une relation significative. Cependant selon d'autres, la relation ne l'est pas (Wallace et *al.,* 1994). Les entreprises appartenant au secteur des hautes technologies sont davantage incitées à la publication d'informations plus fréquemment que les entreprises faisant partie d'autres secteurs. Ceci peut être justifié par le fait que ce secteur est sujet à une volatilité des prix et à une fluctuation importante des bénéfices. Verrecchia (1983) a montré que les coûts indirects de diffusion d'informations privées varient selon les secteurs d'activité. Marston et Leow (1998) confirment ce résultat. Par contre, Bollen et al. (2006) ont découvert une relation négative entre le niveau de technologie et l'ampleur de la diffusion d'informations sur le net. Cependant, Craven et Marston (1999) montrent que la différence entre ces entreprises appartenant à des secteurs industriels différents en matière des mécanismes d'informations n'est pas statistiquement significative.

La cotation sur le marché américain : La divulgation d'informations est influencée par les exigences de cotation sur les marchés financiers ainsi que par les prescriptions des autorités boursières. Plus précisément, par rapport aux marchés de l'Europe continentale, les marchés anglo-saxons sont plus développés et les obligations en termes de communication y sont plus contraignantes (Ding et Stolowy, 2003). Lorsqu'une entreprise est cotée sur les marchés américains, elle doit se conformer aux exigences de ces marchés et publier ses comptes selon les *US GAAP*.

Lakhal (2006) et Leuz et Verrecchia (2001) affirment que la cotation sur le marché américain est l'une des caractéristiques essentielles permettant d'influencer positivement le niveau de la divulgation d'informations. Nous nous attendions à une relation positive entre la cotation sur le marché américain et l'étendue de la divulgation d'informations. La cotation est une variable muette prenant la valeur 1 si l'entreprise est cotée sur le marché américain et 0 sinon.

2. Échantillon et méthodologie

Collecte des données

Notre étude porte sur les entreprises françaises cotées sur la bourse de Paris. L'échantillon de départ était composé de 469 entreprises pour les années 2008 et 2009. L'ensemble des entreprises financières a été écarté vu que ces dernières sont assujetties à des réglementations spécifiques. De même, l'importance des données manquantes et indisponibles nous a obligés à renoncer à une grande partie de notre échantillon initial. L'échantillon final est composé de 155 entreprises dont les données ont été collectées auprès de plusieurs bases de données. Les bases de données *Thomson Reutres* et *Orbis* ont été utilisées pour rassembler les données financières ainsi que les rapports annuels des entreprises. Les informations concernant les mécanismes de gouvernance ont été partiellement récoltées via ces bases. En outre, les bases de données *Dafsaliens*, *Who's Who*[4], et les *États-majors* ont constitué un complément indispensable pour cerner l'expertise et l'indépendance des administrateurs. Les sites Web institutionnels de notre échantillon sont évalués à partir de début du mois de Novembre jusqu'à la fin du mois de Décembre de chaque année.

[4] Le Who's Who (Editions Jacques Lafitte) contient des notices bibliographiques sur un certain nombre de personnes en France. Nous avons eu recours à la version disponible sur internet (www.whoswho.fr) pour obtenir la biographie de plusieurs administrateurs faisant partie de notre échantillon.

Tableau 7.1 Répartition sectorielle de l'échantillon selon la classification ICB[5]

Secteur	ICB Industry code (Thomson Financial Reuters)	Nombre d'entreprises
Matériaux de base	1000	16
Industries	2000	25
Biens de consommation	3000	24
Santé	4000	23
Services aux consommateurs	5000	24
Télécommunications	6000	7
Services aux collectivités	7000	11
Technologie	9000	25
Total 155		155

L'étendue de la divulgation d'informations

Le niveau de publication renvoie à deux dimensions, à savoir la quantité et la qualité des informations véhiculées au public. La qualité des divulgations fait référence à ses attributs. Elle s'exprime en termes de fiabilité, d'intelligibilité, de pertinence et de précision. La quantité des divulgations s'apprécie par le nombre d'informations communiquées. L'étude des caractéristiques de la divulgation d'informations s'appuie sur l'élaboration d'un indice de divulgation. L'objectif est de disposer d'un score global lui-même élaboré par sommation de scores partiels.

Notre indice reflète la dimension quantité. Elle s'apprécie par le nombre d'informations communiquées. Plus l'indice est élevé, plus l'environnement informationnel de l'entreprise est riche. Ainsi l'entreprise est jugée comme étant transparente.

Se basant sur la multi-dimensionnalité de la communication financière de l'entreprise, nous allons utiliser deux supports de publication : le rapport annuel et le site Web institutionnel des entreprises. Notre sélection de ces supports est justifiée par leur privilège dans les milieux financiers.

Le site Web : Internet, véritable outil de gestion de la relation investisseur, permet ainsi à la communauté financière et au public investisseur d'évaluer les entreprises à l'aide des informations mises à leur disposition (Barredy et Darras, 2008). A cet égard, la mise à disposition

---

[5] La nomenclature ICB « Industry Classification Benchmark », qui a été lancée en janvier 2005 par FTSE Group et Dow Jones Indexes, est entrée en service le 2 janvier 2006 pour l'ensemble des sociétés cotées à Amsterdam, Bruxelles, Lisbonne et Paris.

des comptes annuels et autres informations financières sur le site de l'entreprise devient incontournable. La mesure du niveau de divulgation par l'indice est la méthode la plus appropriée (Cooke, 1989 ; Botosan, 1997 ; Marston et Polei, 2004 ; Xiao et *al*, 2004).

L'indice retenu est composé d'items relatifs au contenu et à la forme de présentation des informations sur le web. Le score total représente le nombre des informations publiées par les entreprises et le score théorique correspond au score maximal qu'aurait pu obtenir chaque entreprise. En se référant aux études antérieures (Marston et Polei, 2004 ; Xiao et *al*, 2004), nous avons procédé par une grille d'analyse pour évaluer le niveau de la diffusion volontaire d'informations sur Internet.

Le rapport annuel : Lang et Lundholm (2003) montrent que l'étendue de la publication financière des entreprises est liée positivement au niveau d'informations contenues dans leurs rapports annuels. De surcroît, le rapport annuel est généralement considéré comme l'un des meilleurs supports de communication. Ceci apparaît clairement dans les propos de Knutson (1992)[6]. Notre indice est inspiré des études de Botosan (1997)[7] et Eng et Mak (2003). Notons que ces indices ont été guidés selon les recommandations fournies dans le rapport de Jenkins (AICP[8], 1994) et le Financial Analysts Federation. Les items formant l'indice de divulgation sur ce support sont au nombre de 112 et sont classés en trois catégories (annexe): (1) les informations stratégiques (l'histoire de l'entreprise, sa structure organisationnelle, son activité, ses principaux produits et marchés, sa stratégie actuelle et future et ses perspectives d'avenir ; 30 items), (2) les informations non financières (le nombre et la rémunération des employés de l'entreprise, la valeur ajoutée par employé et les indicateurs de productivité ; 46 items), et (3) les informations financières (les indicateurs de performance autres que ceux obtenus à partir des états financiers, les ratios financiers, les prévisions et d'autres informations financières utiles ; 36 items).

La procédure de mesure de cet indice est bien définie. En effet, il s'agit de lire ces deux supports et d'établir un score total et des sous-scores en divisant le total des points de chaque catégorie par le nombre total des items, selon une échelle bien définie.

---

[6] Knutson (1992): *« At the top of every analyst's list (of financial reports used by analysts) is the annual report to shareholders. It is the major reporting document and every other financial report is in some respect subsidiary or supplementary to it".*

[7] Botosan (1997), qui a publié une des études les plus célèbres en la matière, se contente d'évaluer l'étendue des publications des seuls rapports annuels.

[8] The American Institute of Public Accountants.

Méthodologie

La méthodologie utilisée repose sur les régressions multiples avec des données de panel. La spécificité des analyses en données de panel, c'est qu'elles intègrent deux dimensions : une dimension individuelle, indiquée par l'indice i, représentant l'entreprise, et une dimension temporelle, désignée par l'indice t, et indiquant la période de l'étude considérée. L'un des avantages essentiels des données de panel sur les autres types de données (séries temporelles et coupes transversales) est de permettre de contrôler l'hétérogénéité des observations dans leurs dimensions individuelles, soit par la prise en compte d'un effet spécifique supposé certain, soit par la prise en compte d'un effet spécifique non observable (Gujarati, 2004). Nous utilisons le test de Hausman[9] afin de choisir entre les modèles à effets fixes et les modèles à effets aléatoires et de vérifier le modèle le plus approprié aux données. Un test d'homogénéité a précédé le test de Hausman et a consisté à confirmer la présence des effets individuels dans nos données. Le résultat du test de Hausmann est une loi du Chi deux avec k-1 degrés de liberté. Le résultat de ce test non reporté affiche une probabilité inférieure à 5%. Ceci implique que le modèle à effets fixes est préférable au modèle à effets aléatoires.

Notre méthode consiste en premier lieu à régresser les variables relatives aux caractéristiques du conseil d'administration sur les indices de publication des rapports annuels, des sites Web et du score global. En second lieu, et afin de répondre à nos hypothèses relatives aux caractéristiques du comité d'audit, nous régressons les variables en question sur les mêmes indices de publication.

Analyse et discussion des résultats

Analyse descriptive

Avant d'entamer l'analyse multivariée, nous décrivons d'abord les caractéristiques du conseil d'administration des entreprises de notre échantillon (tableau 2).

---

[9] Le test d'Hausman est un test de spécification qui permet de déterminer si les coefficients des deux estimations (fixe et aléatoire) sont statistiquement différents. L'idée de ce test est que, sous l'hypothèse nulle d'indépendance entre les erreurs et les variables explicatives, les deux estimateurs sont non biaisés, donc les coefficients estimés devraient peu différer. Le test d'Hausman compare la matrice de variance-covariance des deux estimateurs : $W = (\beta f-\beta a)'[var\ (\beta f-\beta a)]^{-1}(\beta f-\beta a)$ Avec : βf est l'estimateur avec effets fixes ; βa est l'estimateur avec effets aléatoires.

Tableau 7.2 Statistiques descriptives[1] :

	adm_taille	*adm_indep*	*adm_exp*	*adm_anc*	*adm_reu*	*Ca_taille*	*Ca_reu*	*Ca_indep*	*Ca_expert*
Mean	8,6	0,33	0,50	5,44	6,47	2,07	2,39	0,33	0,38
Median	8,00	0,33	0,50	4,75	6,00	2,00	2,00	0,25	0,33
Maximum	21,00	1,00	1,00	19,60	22,00	10	12,00	1,00	1,00
Minimum	3,00	0,00	0,03	0,00	2,00	1	0,00	0,00	0,00
Std. Dev.	4,25	0,23	0,19	3,92	3,16	1,75	2,66	0,37	0,37
Skewness	0,62	0,26	0,21	1,16	1,81	7,34	1,04	0,55	0,30
Kurtosis	2,52	2,51	2,42	4,39	8,14	10,15	3,86	1,83	1,60
	Dualité	***Audit***	***BIG4***						
Fréquence	0,54	0,56	0,72						

[1] adm_taille = taille du conseil d'administration; adm_indep : % des administrateurs indépendants ; adm_exp : % des membres expert s financiers dans le conseil d'administration; Dualité = 1 si le directeur général n'occupe pas le poste de président du conseil et zéro s i non. adm_anc : l'ancienneté moyenne des membres du conseil d'administration ; adm_reu : le nombre des réunions du conseil d'ad ministration ; Ca_taille : taille du comité d'audit interne ; Ca_reu : nombre de réunions de comité d'audit ; Ca_indep : la proportion d es administrateurs indépendants ; Ca_expert : la proportion des administrateurs experts financiers.

Les différentes variables choisies justifient en général l'inexistence d'un consensus clair et d'un standard pour la gouvernance d'entreprise française. L'absence de lois régissant les proportions minimales, les quotas, et l'activité des différentes caractéristiques de gouvernance prises dans cette étude traduisent une souplesse législative française qui continue à influencer les pratiques de gouvernance malgré l'adoption de la loi du 3 juillet 2008[1].

Le problème de corrélation tient au fait que certaines variables explicatives sont liées les unes aux autres, ou « s'expliquent » partiellement les unes les autres. Elles offrent alors une explication redondante de la variable dépendante. Ce problème, connu sous le terme de multicolinéarité, rend instables et peu fiables les coefficients de régression des variables corrélées entre elles, puisque leurs effets s'empiètent les uns sur les autres. Pour analyser les liaisons entre ces variables, il est fréquent d'utiliser les coefficients de corrélation de *Pearson.* Une analyse bi-variée a été conduite pour tester l'éventuelle présence d'un problème de multi colinéarité entre les variables explicatives.

Analyse multivariée et discussion

Les résultats du tableau 4 mettent en évidence une relation positive non significative entre la taille du conseil d'administration et l'indice de publication des rapports annuels. Le même résultat, mais cette fois significatif, est trouvé avec le score des sites web et le score total. Ce résultat est justifié par la théorie de la dépendance envers les ressources, qui stipule que l'amélioration des relations des entreprises avec les différentes parties prenantes est rendue possible dans le cadre de conseils élargis. Chtourou, Bédard et Courteau (2001) et Anderson et *al.* (2004) ont abouti à des résultats similaires aux nôtres.

La proportion des administrateurs indépendants ainsi que la proportion des membres experts financiers dans le conseil d'administration ne semblent pas avoir de liens significatifs avec l'étendue de la divulgation d'informations. Par ailleurs, les résultats montrent que le nombre des réunions du conseil d'administration et l'ancienneté moyenne des membres contribuent à l'amélioration du niveau de publication d'informations. Ce résultat confirme nos quatrième et cinquième hypothèses et rejoint celui

---

[1] Les articles 26 à 30 de la loi du 03 juillet 2008 visent à accroitre les obligations de transparence des sociétés en matière de gouvernement d'entreprise et de contrôle interne. Ces sociétés se trouvent obligés de préciser le code de gouvernement d'entreprise auquel la société a choisi de se référer ou, à défaut, les règles retenues par cette société en complément des exigences requises par la loi.

trouvé par Koppes et *al.,* (1999) et Jenkins (2002). L'ancienneté des membres renforce leur capacité à exercer un contrôle sur la haute direction. Plus les administrateurs sont expérimentés, plus leur mandat est assuré au sein de l'entreprise, et moins la probabilité d'émettre des états financiers frauduleux et de là, la divulgation d'informations s'améliore.

Nos résultats confortent également la sixième hypothèse selon laquelle il existe une relation négative entre la présence d'une structure moniste et la divulgation d'informations. L'utilisation d'une structure qui dissocie les fonctions de président de conseil et de PDG n'est pas efficace et la transparence de l'information serait menacée. Haniffa et Cooke (2000) trouvent des résultats similaires dans un contexte malaisien.

Les résultats du tableau 4 mettent aussi en exergue l'influence négative de la taille de l'entreprise sur l'étendue de la divulgation d'informations, ce qui contredit nos prédictions. Quant à la performance, telle que mesurée par la rentabilité des capitaux investis, nous montrons qu'elle est positivement associée à la divulgation d'informations appréhendée par les trois scores. Nous trouvons un effet positif et significatif entre l'étendue des informations publiées et la performance des entreprises. Ce résultat indique que les entreprises améliorent leurs mécanismes d'informations pour informer le marché des bonnes performances de l'entreprise. Paturel et al. (2006) pensent également que plus l'entreprise est performante plus le niveau d'informations publiées sera élevé.

Le coefficient de la variable secteur apparaît positif et statistiquement significatif au seuil de 5%. Le signe positif de ce coefficient valide notre hypothèse dans le sens où l'appartenance au secteur haute technologie affecte positivement le score en matière de divulgation d'informations sur les rapports annuels et internet. Ce résultat rejoint ceux de Debreceny et *al.* (2002) et de Xiao et *al.* (2004). Dès lors, les entreprises appartenant au secteur haute technologie auraient plus tendance à mieux informer les différentes parties prenantes et exploiter internet et rapports annuels comme mécanismes d'informations. Nous pouvons déceler ici leur désir de démontrer leur expertise en la matière afin de valoriser leur savoir-faire.

A la vue des scores obtenus, nous pouvons remarquer que les entreprises affichant les meilleurs scores sont celles cotées sur le marché américain. Cela peut s'expliquer par le fait que ces entreprises sont les plus grandes et les plus liquides, et qui peuvent produire un niveau élevé d'informations publiées. Ce résultat confirme que les entreprises cotées sur le marché américain sont plus informatives. Ces entreprises adoptent les *US GAAP* américains, plus exigeants en matière d'informations, d'où l'effet positif sur la divulgation d'informations.

Tableau 7.3 Régression des scores de publication : conseil d'administration[2]

	Disc.RA		Disc.SW		Disc.Tot	
Constante	-0,331***	(-9,57)	0,509***	-10,59	1,059***	-9,95
adm_taille	0 ,010	-1,1	0,026**	-2,36	0,062**	-1,96
adm_indep	-0,027	(-0,80)	0,023*	-1,76	0,041	-0,97
adm_exp	0,04	-1,19	-0,015	(-0,64)	0,063	-1,38
adm_anc	0,05***	-2,95	0,017**	-2,13	0,091***	-4,06
adm_reu	0,112***	-4,69			0,064**	-2,12
Dual	-0,067***	(-4,49)	-0,011*	(-1,88)	-0,099***	(-5,73)
Taille	-0,044	(-1,32)	-0,011	(-0,38)	-0,02	(-1.57)
ROE	0,853*	-1,88	0,214	-1,22	0,972**	-1,99
Secteur	0,039**	-2,13	0,017**	-2,21	0,026	-1,2
USCOT	0,021	-1,27	0,038***	-4,86	0,062***	-3,28
R^2	0,14		0,18		0,14	
F-statistic	6,21 (0,000)		7,38 (0,000)		7,90(0,000)	

Conclusion

La politique de la divulgation d'informations est souvent perçue comme un moyen efficace d'atténuation de l'asymétrie informationnelle subséquente à l'accès aux marchés financiers (Healy et Palepu, 2001). Elle est également justifiée par la volonté d'abaisser le coût du capital lié aux opérations de financement (Botosan, 1997 ; Botosan et Plumlee, 2000). Dans ce cadre, l'objectif principal de notre recherche était principalement d'analyser les facteurs relatifs aux mécanismes de gouvernance qui déterminent l'étendue de la communication financière. Nous avons appréhendé la divulgation d'informations des entreprises étudiées, en exploitant l'apport crucial au courant de recherche consacré aux scores ou indices de divulgation. Ces indices sont calculés sur la base de deux

[2] Disc.RA Indice de divulgation du rapport annuel ; Disc.SW : Indice de divulgatio n du site Web ; Disc.Tot : Indice de divulgation total ; adm_taille = taille du conseil d'administration mesurée par le nombre total des administrateurs ; adm_act = pour centage des actions détenues par les administrateurs ; adm_indep : % des administr ateurs indépendants ; adm_exp : % des membres experts financiers dans un conseil d'administration; Dual = 1 si le directeur général n'occupe pas le poste de présiden t du conseil et zéro si non. adm_anc : l'ancienneté moyenne des membres du conse il d'administration ; adm_reu : le nombre des réunions du conseil d'administratio n ; *Taille :* Taille de l'entreprise ; *ROE :* Performance de l'entreprise ; *Secteur :* Sec teur d'activité ; *USCOT :* Cotation sur le marché américain.

supports jugés les plus importants par les investisseurs en termes de recherche d'informations, à savoir le rapport annuel et le site Web.

Plus spécifiquement, sur la base d'un échantillon de 155 entreprises non financières et pour deux ans, nous avons testé l'impact des caractéristiques du conseil d'administration et du comité d'audit sur l'étendue de la divulgation d'informations, en se basant sur les hypothèses de la théorie de l'agence, la théorie de l'enracinement et la théorie de l'intendance. Les résultats obtenus ont permis de conclure une relation positive entre la taille du conseil d'administration et le score des sites web reflétant l'étendue de la divulgation d'informations.

Par ailleurs, les résultats montrent que l'ancienneté moyenne des membres du conseil d'administration, le nombre des réunions du conseil d'administration et le cumul des rôles de chef de direction et du président du conseil contribuent à l'amélioration du niveau de publication d'informations. Néanmoins, les variables : proportion des administrateurs indépendants et proportion des membres experts financiers dans le conseil d'administration, ne semblent pas avoir un effet significatif. Les résultats sont quasiment pareils pour les trois scores utilisés, à savoir le score des rapports annuels, des sites Web ou bien le score global. Ces résultats sont convergents avec les études antérieures. Il reste à noter enfin que les entreprises françaises doivent renforcer la crédibilité de leur système de gouvernance. En effet, la transparence du marché français doit passer par la mise en place de plus de contraintes sur ce système. Ces contraintes sont spécifiquement liées aux caractéristiques du conseil d'administration et du comité de vérification. Bien que les conclusions de ce papier et d'autres études examinées aillent généralement dans le même sens, il en ressort que les écarts de conduite des entreprises en matière de transparence sont souvent associés aux mauvaises pratiques de gouvernance que les réformes actuelles tentent de corriger.

Bibliographie

Abbott J., Parker S. (2004), « Audit committee characteristics and restatements », *Auditing: A Journal of Practice and Theory*, Vol. 23, p. 69-87

Agrawal A., Knoeber C. (1999). Firm performance and mechanisms to control agency problems between managers and shareholders. *Journal of financial and quantitative analysis*, Vol. 31, p. 377-397.

Anderson D., Francis R., Stokes J. (1993), « Auditing Directorship and Demand for Monitoring », *Journal of Accounting and Public Policy*, Vol. 12, p. 353-375.

Anderson R., Mansi S., David R. (2004), « Board characteristics, accounting report integrity, and cost of debt », *Journal of Accounting and Economies*, Vol. 37, p. 315-342.

Attig N. (2007), « Family pyramidal holdings and board of directors », *International Journal of Business Governance and Ethics*, Vol. 3, p. 394-406.

Beasley M. (1996), « An empirical analysis of the relation between the Board of director composition and financial statement fraud », *The Accounting Review*, Vol. 71, p. 433-465.

Cai C., Keasey K., Short H., (2006), « Corporate Governance and Information Efficiency in Security Markets », *European Financial Management*, Vol. 12, p. 763-787.

Chae J. (2005), « Timing information, information asymmetry, and trading volume », *The Journal of Finance*, Vol. 61, p.413-442.

Charoenwong C., Ding D., Visaltanachoti N. (2010), « Adverse selection and corporate governance », *International Review of Economics and Finance.*

Charreaux G., Pitol Belin P. (1990), « Le conseil d'administration», Vuibert

Chen, J., Jaggi B, (2000), « Association between Independent Non-Executive Directors, Family Control and Financial Disclosures in Hong Kong », *Journal of Accounting and Public Policy*, Vol. 19, p. 285-310.

Dahya J., Dimitrov O., and McConnell J. (2008), « Dominant shareholders, corporate boards, and corporate value: A cross-country analysis », *Journal of Financial Economics*, Vol.87, p. 73-100.

Davis J.H., Schoorman F.D. et Donaldson L. (1997), « Towards a stewardship theory of management », *Academy of Management Review*, 1997, vol. 22, n° 1, pp. 20-47.

Deangelio L. (1988), « Managerial competition, information costs and corporate governance: the use of accounting performance measures in proxy contests», *Journal of Accounting and Economies*, Vol. 10, p. 3-36.

Dechow P., Sloan R., Sweenny A. (1996), « Causes and Consequences of Earning Manipulations: An Analysis of Firm Subject to Enforcement Actions by the SEC », *Contemporary Accounting Research*, Vol. 13, p. 1-136.

Defond L., Jiambalvo J. (1993), « Factors Related to Auditor- Client Disagreements over Income-Increasing Accounting Methods », *Contemporary Accounting Research*, Vol. 9, p. 415-431.

Edwards A., Harris L., Piwowar M. (2007). Corporate bond market transaction costs and transparency. *The Journal of Finance Vol.* 62.

Eng L., Mak Y. (2003), « Corporate governance and voluntary disclosure », *Journal of Accounting and Public Policy*, vol.22, p. 325-345.

Fama E. (1980), «Agency Problems and the Theory of the Firm», *Journal of Political Economy*, n°88, p. 288-307.

Fama E., Jensen M. (1983), « Separation of Ownership and Control », *Journal of Law and Economics*, p. 301-326.

Glosten L., Milgrom P. (1985), « Bid, Ask and Transaction Prices in a Specialist Market with Heterogeneously Informed Traders », *Journal of Financial Economics*, Vol.14, p. 71-100.

Godar L., Schatt A., (2000), « Faut-il limiter le cumul des fonctions dans les conseils d'administration ? », *La Revue du Financier*, Vol. 127, p. 36-47.

Hamon J., Jacquillat B. (1992), « Le marché français des actions. Études empiriques 1977-1991 », Collection finance, PUF.

Haniffa R., T. Cooke T. (2000), « Culture, corporate governance and disclosure in Malaysian corporations », *Working paper.*

Heflin F., Shaw W., Wild J. (2005), « Disclosure policy and market liquidity: Impact of depth quotes and order sizes », *Contemporary Accounting Research*, Vol. 22, p.829-866

Ho, S, Wong S., (2001), « A study of the relationship between corporate governance structure and the extent of voluntary disclosure », *Journal of International Accounting, Auditing and Taxation*, Vol. 10, p. 139-156

Jeanjean T., Stolowy H., (2009), « Determinants of board members' financial expertise: Empirical evidence from France », *International Journal of Accounting*, Vol. 44, p. 378-402

Jensen M. (1993), « The modem industrial revolution, Exit, and Failure of the international control Systems », *Journal of Finance*, Vol 20, p. 831-830

Jensen M., and Meckling W. (1976), «Theory of the Firm: Managerial Behavior, Agency Costs, and Ownership Structure», *Journal of Financial Economics*, p. 305-360

Kanagaretnam K., Lobo J., Whalen J., (2007), « Does good corporate governance reduce information asymmetry around quarterly earnings announcements? », *Journal of Accounting and Public Policy*, Vol.26, p. 497-522

Klein A. (2002), « Audit Committee, Board of Director Characteristics, and Earnings Management », *Journal of Accounting and Economics*, Vol. 33, p. 375-400

Koppes H., Ganske G., Charles H. (1999), « Corporate governance out of focus: The debate over classified boards », *the business lawyer*, Vol. 54, 1023-1055

Kyle A. (1985), « Continuous Auctions and Insider Trading », *Econometrica*, Vol. 53, p. 1315-1335

Leuz C., Verrecchia R. (2000), « The economic consequences of increased disclosure », *Journal of Accounting Research,* Vol. 38, p.91-124

Lin C., Sanger G., Booth G. (1995), « Trade size and the components of the bid ask spread », *Review of financial studies*, Vol.8, p.1153-1183.

MEDEF (2003), « Le gouvernement d'entreprise des sociétés cotées », MEDEF

Prat C., Komarev I., (2005), « Légitimité et exigences réglementaires au sein de la gouvernance des sociétés cotées américaines et françaises : les comités d'audit », La *Revue Française des Sciences de gestion*, Vol.40, p.33-47.

Pfeffer J. et Salancik G.R., (1978), « The external control of organizations: a resource dependence perspective », *Harper & Row,* New York

Raghunandan K., William R. (2001), « Audit committee composition, "gray directors," and interaction with internal auditing », *Accounting Horizons*, Vol. 15.

Ross S., (1977) « The determination of financial structure: the incentive signalling approach », *Bell Journal of Economics*, vol 8, printemps, p. 23-40

Schauer P. 2002, « The effects of industry specialization on audit quality: an examination using bid-ask spreads », *Journal of Accounting and Finance Research*, Vol 10, p. 76-86

Shleifer A., Vishny R. (1989), « Management Entrenchment: The Case of Manager Specific Investments », *Journal of Financial Economics*, n° 2, p. 123-139

Whittington G., (1993), « Corporate governance and the regulation of financial reporting », *Accounting and Business Research,* Vol. 23, p. 311-319

Xiao J., Yang H., Chow C. (2004), « The Determinants And Characteristics of Voluntary Internet-based Disclosure By Listed Chinese Companies », *Journal of Accounting and Public Policy*, Vol. 23, p.191-225.

GOUVERNANCE ET ENTREPRENEURIAT SOCIAL : LE CAS DES SCOP EN FRANCE

LAURICE ALEXANDRE-LECLAIR

Résumé

Dans le cadre d'une économie sociale et solidaire, l'entrepreneuriat social paraît comme la pratique la plus courue du 21ème siècle, notamment grâce à sa gouvernance participative et à son rôle dans le développement économique et social. Le profil juridique des employeurs du secteur varie entre coopératives, mutuelles, associations, et fondations. Dans notre article, nous étudions le cas des sociétés de coopération et de participation (SCOP) car ce sont les seules structures qui représentent une gouvernance participative et démocratique à la fois. Notre recherche se base essentiellement sur une étude de cas approfondie d'une SCOP dans le domaine du Conseil en Management.

Mots clés : entrepreneuriat social, gouvernance, participation, coopératives, Scop.

Introduction

Constituée d'associations, coopératives, mutuelles et fondations, l'économie sociale et solidaire (ESS) rassemble les structures qui se définissent, par leur statut, comme des groupements de personnes et non de capitaux (Observatoire national de l'Economie sociale et solidaire, 2012). En France l'ESS concerne 10% environ de l'emploi français, 215000 établissements employeurs, et plus de 100000 emplois créés chaque année. D'après le CNCRES1 (2012) (données 2008), ce sont les associations qui occupent la forme juridique la plus courante dans ce secteur avec 80% du volume d'emplois, suivies par les coopératives qui représentent 12%. Alors que la taille moyenne d'une entreprise du secteur d'ESS est de 11 salariés, elle est de 9 salariés pour les PME du secteur privé hors ESS. Ce qui démontre la croissance du secteur et son rôle comme un moteur pour l'emploi. D'ailleurs, le taux de croissance des emplois dans le secteur a été de 2,4% en 2008 contre 1,8% pour le secteur privé. Quant au secteur d'activité concerné par l'ESS, c'est le secteur tertiaire qui regroupe la majorité des effectifs salariés (associations, mutuelles et fondations), alors que les coopératives exercent essentiellement dans des activités de production : industrie, construction, et agriculture. Nous signalons enfin que l'emploi des femmes est majoritaire (66%) dans l'économie sociale et solidaire.

Bien que les coopératives occupent un pourcentage faible par rapport aux associations, nous avons choisi les coopératives comme sujet de discussion pour notre article, car c'est au sein de ces structures que la gouvernance participative et surtout démocratique culmine. En effet, les entreprises coopératives, en conciliant valeurs économiques et sociales, et grâce à un fonctionnement spécifique, résistent mieux à la crise : la maitrise du capital par les membres associés, une gouvernance démocratique, un centre de décision ancré localement, des résultats qui restent dans l'entreprise, des réserves financières impartageables, une stratégie tournée vers le long terme avec des profits qui servent d'abord la pérennité de la coopérative, etc. L'ensemble des entreprises coopératives affiche un poids socio-économique important, avec 21 000 entreprises en France qui emploient près d'un million de salariés. Près de 24 millions de membres font vivre la gouvernance démocratique des entreprises coopératives françaises.

En 2010, elles ont réalisé 288 milliards de chiffre d'affaires cumulé, filiales comprises, en augmentation de 31 milliards d'euros depuis 2009, soit +5,1%. Enfin, elles sont présentes, et parfois leaders, dans tous les secteurs d'activité (agriculture, artisanat, banque, commerce, consommation, culture, éducation, industrie, logement, NTIC, pêche, recherche, services, transport, etc.) (Rapport du conseil supérieur de la coopération, 2007). Cela dit, les coopératives pouvant prendre plusieurs formes juridiques, et ne pouvant être exhaustive, nous traiterons uniquement le cas des SCOP (sociétés de coopération et de participation) car c'est la forme la plus représentative de la gouvernance participative et démocratique.

Les Scop sont des entreprises à part entière, présentes sur l'économie de marché et exposées pleinement à la concurrence. Elles sont confrontées à l'impératif de profitabilité. Mais ce qui les distingue est l'utilisation de leurs profits, tournés en priorité vers les salariés et la pérennité de l'entreprise, sans oublier de rémunérer le capital. (les-scop.coop, 2012). Il est possible d'entreprendre en Scop dans tous les métiers. Aujourd'hui, un tiers des emplois de Scop sont dans le BTP, un quart dans l'industrie et plus de 40% sont dans les services de toutes natures.

Les Scop connaissent un développement régulier en France depuis plus de quinze ans. Tous métiers confondus, leur chiffre d'affaires et leur valeur ajoutée ont doublé en 10 ans. Le taux de survie des entreprises créées en Scop s'élève à 57% en comparaison à la moyenne nationale qui est de 52% (source INSEE). Dans l'industrie, les Scop ont mieux résisté, depuis dix ans, que les autres PME grâce à leur gouvernance coopérative. Tournées vers le métier, les employés et le long terme, les Scop développent leur chiffre d'affaires sur une base capitalistique solides.

Ainsi, après une première partie explicative sur l'entrepreneuriat social et les Scop, nous présenterons dans la deuxième partie une étude de cas sur une SCOP (ATARAXIA) spécialisée dans le Management et l'organisation.

1. L'entrepreneuriat social dans une économie sociale et solidaire

Entrepreneuriat et utilité sociale

Le Mouvement des entrepreneurs sociaux définit les entreprises sociales comme « des entreprises à finalité sociale, sociétale ou environnementale et à lucrativité limitée. Ancrée dans les valeurs de l'économie sociale et solidaire, elles cherchent à associer leurs parties prenantes à leur gouvernance » (Mouves.fr). Johnson (2000), estime de son côté que *« L'entrepreneuriat social* fait éclater les frontières traditionnelles entre le secteur public, le privé et le non-lucratif et met en avant des modèles hybrides d'activités lucratives et non lucratives ».

Dans la même lignée Townsend, et Hart (2008) déclarent que « L'entrepreneuriat émerge comme une approche commune visant à répondre aux besoins sociaux. Toutefois les créateurs s'organisent tout aussi bien sous une forme lucrative non lucrative afin de s'engager vers des activités relativement similaires ». Par ailleurs, Gadrey (2004) définit l'utilité sociale comme étant « l'activité d'une organisation qui contribue à la cohésion sociale (notamment par la réduction des inégalités), à la solidarité (nationale, internationale, ou locale) et à la sociabilité, et à l'amélioration des conditions collectives du développement humain durable dont font partie l'éducation, la santé, l'environnement et la démocratie ». Cela dit, selon l'instruction fiscale, une association ou entreprise est considéré à utilité sociale selon les 4 P suivants :

a) Le Produit proposé répond à un besoin peu ou mal pris en considération par le marché ;

b) Le public visé est constitué de personnes que le marché délaisse ou dont la situation économique et sociale justifie l'octroi d'avantages particuliers ;

c) La publicité est réduite à des opérations de communication ;

d) Le prix se distingue de ceux pratiqués par le secteur lucratif grâce à l'effort consenti pour faciliter l'accès du public.

Comme nous le constatons, la gouvernance participative est au cœur de l'entrepreneuriat social. Cela dit, bien que la participation soit basée sur le principe « d'une personne, une voix », son application varie selon le statut de l'entreprise. D'après notre recherche, nous constatons que la gouvernance participative la plus démocratique concernait plutôt les Scop, car les dirigeants des SCOP, en créant leurs sociétés, font le choix de partager le capital avec les salariés mais aussi et surtout de rester dans une politique de lucrativité limitée. Nous traitons ces aspects dans la partie suivante.

De l'actionnariat salarié à la SCOP

Rojot (2010), caractérise l'actionnariat salarié par deux volets : d'une part, la participation aux profits ou à toute autre forme de résultats de l'entreprise encadrée par les textes de 1959 et de 1967, portant respectivement sur la «participation aux fruits de l'expansion» et «l'intéressement», modifiés depuis à de multiples reprises. Et d'autre part, la participation à la propriété de l'entreprise au-delà du seul (éventuel) profit. L'actionnariat salarié se distingue encore d'une autre forme de participation financière, illustrée par les anciennes sociétés coopératives ouvrières de production (SCOP). Il existe une ambiguïté entre actionnariat salarié et coopérative de production illustrée par la loi du 26 avril 1917 qui réglementait les sociétés anonymes à participation ouvrière et qui avait, dans une version différente, failli constituer un volet de la loi de 1864 sur les sociétés. Mais les deux concepts doivent être clairement distingués. Certes, dans les deux cas, tout ou partie des salariés sont propriétaires des actions de tout ou partie de l'entreprise. L'actionnaire salarié est propriétaire d'actions de la société dans laquelle il travaille, soumises au régime général des actions de société, cessibles sinon toujours négociables, alors que le salarié coopérateur ne peut céder ses actions qu'à la société coopérative, et à un prix généralement inchangé par rapport au prix d'acquisition.

En outre, l'actionnaire salarié dispose du droit de vote représenté par les actions qu'il possède en assemblée générale, alors que le salarié coopérateur se voit appliquer le principe «un homme, une voix», et que les salariés coopérateurs sont toujours majoritaires dans une SCOP. Il ne s'agit donc pas du même dispositif. D'un point de vue juridique, dans le cadre de l'actionnariat salarié, le salarié est actionnaire de sa propre entreprise et soumis au droit du travail et au droit des sociétés. La Fédération française des associations d'actionnaires salariés et anciens salariés (FAS) réserve le qualificatif d'actionnaire salarié à «un actionnaire qui a investi volontairement, à long terme, une partie de son épargne en titres de son entreprise, de façon directe ou indirecte, dans le cadre d'opérations spécifiques réservées à tous les salariés, en souhaitant s'impliquer davantage dans son entreprise et en lui accordant sa confiance».

Historique et fonctionnement des SCOP :

« Au cours des trois premiers quarts du 19ème siècle, les ouvriers cherchent à défendre leur droit au travail et leur autonomie. Des associations ouvrières sont créées de façon clandestine, la loi Le Chapelier de 1791 les interdisant. Les apports de théoriciens et de praticiens utopistes, popularisant les idées de communauté et de démocratie, ont contribué à faire émerger le mouvement de la coopération de production. Parmi les plus célèbres : Saint-Simon, Charles Fourier, Jean-Baptiste Godin, Louis Blanc, Philippe Buchez, Jeanne Deroin, Joseph Proudhon, Robert Owen (Angleterre) » (source les-scop.coop.fr). D'après la même source, 1831 fut l'année du premier contrat « d'association des travailleurs » établi par des menuisiers dans le but d'améliorer leurs conditions de travail. Le statut des salariés n'a pas cessé d'évoluer depuis, et les coopératives ont pris de plus en plus de l'ampleur. C'est en 1915 que les textes concernant les SCOP (société coopérative de production » a vu le jour dans le livre III du code du travail. Et c'est en 2010 que l'appellation « Société coopérative et participative », remplace l'ancienne appellation « coopérative ouvrière de production ». Les SCOP, **Sociétés coopératives et participatives**, désignent les entreprises à statut SCOP (Société coopérative de production (ancienne appellation)) et à statut SCOP (Société coopérative d'intérêt collectif). Soumises à l'impératif de profitabilité comme toute entreprise, elles bénéficient d'une gouvernance démocratique et d'une répartition des résultats prioritairement affectée à la pérennité des emplois et du projet d'entreprise.

Les deux formes juridiques de Sociétés coopératives et participatives :

La SCOP

Juridiquement, une SCOP est une société coopérative de forme SA ou SARL dont les salariés sont les associés majoritaires et détiennent au moins 51 % du capital social et 65 % des droits de vote. Si tous les salariés ne sont pas associés, tous ont vocation à le devenir. Le dirigeant est élu par les salariés associés. Cela dit, seules les grandes décisions stratégiques sont prises avec l'ensemble des salariés associés lors des Assemblées générales. Au quotidien, le dirigeant assume pleinement son rôle. D'autant plus que ce sont les salariés eux-mêmes qui l'ont choisi. Les rapports sociaux sont par conséquent plus équilibrés entre salariés et dirigeants. Dans la pratique, la durée moyenne d'exercice d'un dirigeant de SCOP est d'une vingtaine d'années environ.

Les dirigeants de SCOP n'ont pas de bonus ou de stock-options, mais leur valeur est reconnue. Une SCOP s'inscrit dans les politiques de rémunération du marché du travail comme toutes les entreprises. Privilégiant la valeur travail, les SCOP reconnaissent par nature les qualifications et les compétences. La SCOP est la seule coopérative dont les membres associés sont les salariés. Dans une coopérative agricole ou une coopérative de consommateurs, les membres associés ne sont pas les salariés, mais des agriculteurs ou des consommateurs qui mettent en commun leurs ressources. Une SCOP peut accueillir des associés extérieurs qui peuvent détenir jusqu'à 49% du capital et 35% des droits de vote. Au-delà de ces 49%, les associés extérieurs peuvent aussi investir en titres participatifs, qui ne leur donnent pas de droit de vote, mais leur attribuent une rémunération plus forte, composée d'une partie fixe et d'un complément variable d'autant plus élevé que les résultats de l'entreprise sont bons. Dans une SCOP, le partage du profit est équitable :

- une part pour tous les salariés, sous forme de participation et d'intéressement ;
- une part pour les salariés associés sous forme de dividendes ;
- une part pour les réserves de l'entreprise.

Les réserves, impartageables et définitives (en moyenne 40 à 45 % du résultat) vont contribuer tout au long du développement de l'entreprise à consolider les fonds propres et à assurer sa pérennité. Les co-entrepreneurs sont rémunérés de leur travail et de leur apport en capital, mais à leur départ, celui-ci leur est remboursé sans plus-value.

La SCIC

Dans une SCIC, les mécanismes coopératifs et participatifs sont identiques à ceux de la SCOP. Toutefois, les membres associés au capital sont par définition de toutes natures : salariés mais aussi celles et ceux qui souhaitent s'impliquer dans le projet : clients, bénévoles, collectivités territoriales, partenaires privés, etc. Nous rappelons enfin, que pour les deux formes, un homme est équivalent à une voix et que les salariés sont actionnaires ou appelés à le devenir.

Afin d'approfondir le rôle de la gouvernance dans les SCOP et son apport dans le cadre d'une économie sociale et solidaire, nous avons décidé de mener une recherche terrain afin d'évaluer le rôle du dirigeant d'une SCOP dans le bon fonctionnement de son entreprise, dans la motivation des salariés et surtout le management de son équipe.

2. Le fonctionnement des Scop, le cas de l'entreprise ATARAXIA

Avant de présenter les résultats de notre recherche, nous présenterons la méthodologie de recherche adoptée suivie par les résultats obtenus.

Méthodologie de la recherche

Afin de compléter notre recherche bibliographique qui porte sur l'entrepreneuriat social et les SCOP, nous avons débuté une recherche terrain au travers d'une étude de cas auprès de l'entreprise ATARAXIA, entreprise de Conseil en Management et organisation. Jusqu'à présent, nous avons mené deux entretiens individuels avec son directeur général, nous devons rencontrer prochainement ses associés et quelques salariés et mener ainsi, un ou deux « focus group » afin de connaître leurs points de vue sur la gouvernance participative et surtout sur leurs motivations pour rejoindre une SCOP; le choix d'une étude de cas se justifie pour notre problématique qui demeure exploratoire avec un objectif premier qui est de compléter la littérature et surtout l'affronter à la pratique.

Premiers résultats

Le Directeur Général d'ATARAXIA annonce que, basée sur le principe de la coopération, une SCOP ne peut être créée par un seul individu. Il faut être deux associés ou plus pour pouvoir créer une société avec ce statut. Dans leur cas, ils sont 3 actionnaires et il a été élu par les deux autres associés comme Directeur général. Le principe de la démocratie est donc confirmé, ce qui lui confère le rôle de manager, mais cela ne signifie pas que les autres associés ne participent pas aux décisions prises. Il déclare que « le fait d'être élu, cela me donne toute la légitimité et toute la confiance de la part de mes collaborateurs ». Le principe d'une personne, une voix est appliqué, cela « implique les salariés dans leur travail quotidien, dans la mesure où ils se sentent responsables de leur propre entreprise ».

D'autant plus que la lucrativité étant limitée, les associés et les salariés « actionnaires » ont pour objectif commun la prospérité de leur entreprise et le recrutement de nouvelles personnes ayant la même motivation. Dans le sens où le modèle économique de l'entreprise orienté vers la réalisation des profits, mais ces profits sont réinvestis au sein de l'entreprise dans le but d'acheter du matériel mais aussi et surtout pour s'agrandir et assurer une présence et une visibilité sur le marché du travail.

En effet, la motivation principale du directeur général et de ses associés pour créer une SCOP est lié, à l'unanimité, à une déception individuelle, de leurs expériences passées dans un modèle économique capitalistique. Nous avons aussi constaté chez le Directeur Général une sensibilité particulière pour les causes sociales. Cela explique en grande partie le choix de la structure juridique des SCOP, les personnes dirigeant cette forme d'entreprise ne pouvant être attiré par l'enrichissement personnel. D'ailleurs, les salariés recrutés au sein de l'entreprise doivent devenir actionnaires de leur entreprise moyennant une participation obligatoire au capital après une période d'essai. Cette clause fait partie du contrat de travail. Nous compléterons cette partie à la suite des entretiens auprès des associés et des salariés de l'entreprise.

Conclusion

L'entrepreneuriat social, notamment les coopératives ayant le statut SCOP, participe bel et bien au développement économique des entreprises et à la création d'emplois. Sa gouvernance participative et démocratique, orientée vers l'épanouissement de l'individu en creusant dans ses actions dans et envers la société, et non vers l'enrichissement personnel en fait la forme juridique d'excellence dans le cadre d'une stratégie de développement durable et de responsabilité sociale.

Notre recherche comporte néanmoins plusieurs limites. La première concerne la méthodologie adoptée. En effet, une étude de cas unique ne permet pas de comparer ni de généraliser nos résultats. La deuxième concerne la nature des résultats obtenus dans le sens où nous avons adopté une méthode qualitative, mais il serait judiciable de la compléter avec une étude quantitative auprès des différents directeurs de SCOP, leurs associés et leurs salariés, afin d'avoir une vue d'ensemble de la gouvernance dans le secteur et surtout les motivations des différentes parties prenantes.

Bibliographie

Demoustier D. (2001), L'économie sociale et solidaire : s'associer pour entreprendre autrement, Syros.

Gadrey J. (2004) « L'utilité sociale des organisations de l'économie sociale et solidaire », rapport de synthèse pour la DIES et la MIRE.

Johnson S., (2000), *Literature review on social entrepreneurship*, Canadian Centre for Social Entrepreneurship, University of Alberta.

Rojot J. (2010), l'actionnariat salarié, une solution ou un problème ? *in Pierre-Eric Tixier Ressources Humaines pour sortie de crise*, p.p. 171-186.

Townsend D.M., Hart T.A. (2008), « Perceived institutional ambiguity and the choice of organizational form in social entrepreneurial ventures », *Entrepreneurship Theory and Practice*, 32(4), 685-700.

(CNRES, 2012) Panorama de l'économie sociale et solidaire en France et dans les régions, étude réalisée par l'INSEE en collaboration avec le Conseil National des Chambres régionales de l'économie sociale et solidaire.

http://www.Entreprises.Coop (2012), Panorama sectoriel des entreprises coopératives, Top 100 des entreprises coopératives 2012.

Rapport du Conseil supérieur de la coopération (2007), le mouvement coopératif en France.

http//www.mouves.fr

http://www.les-scop.coop 11

Annexe 1 : Historique des SCOP : (source : http://www.scop.coop)

Au cours des trois premiers quarts du 19ème siècle, les ouvriers cherchent à défendre leur droit au travail et leur autonomie. Des associations ouvrières sont créées de façon clandestine, la loi Le Chapelier de 1791 les interdisant. Les apports de théoriciens et de praticiens utopistes, popularisant les idées de communauté et de démocratie, ont contribué à faire émerger le mouvement de la coopération de production. Parmi les plus célèbres : Saint-Simon, Charles Fourier, Jean-Baptiste Godin, Louis Blanc, Philippe Buchez, Jeanne Deroin, Joseph Proudhon, Robert Owen (Angleterre)…

1831 Premier " contrat d'association de travailleurs " établi par des menuisiers avec l'assistance d'un médecin philanthrope Philippe Buchez (Cf art : " Moyen d'améliorer la condition des salariés de villes " paru dans le Journal des sciences morales et politiques).

1834 Création de l'Association des Bijoutiers en Doré, qui avec le " contrat d'association de travailleurs " de Buchez sont les précurseurs de la coopérative de production.

1848 Suite à l'insurrection républicaine déclenchée en février, encouragement par le gouvernement provisoire des associations ouvrières. Puis quelques mois plus tard, persécutions policières contre les associations ouvrières.

1849 Première esquisse de Fédération des Associations Ouvrières (à l'appel de Jeanne Deroin). Ses promoteurs, accusés d'avoir conspiré contre le gouvernement, seront envoyés en prison.

1851 Coup d'Etat du 2 décembre amenant le Second Empire. Les associations ouvrières sont réduites rapidement à néant et leurs militants sont poursuivis et lourdement condamnés.

1864 Abrogation de la loi instituant le délit de coalition.

1867 Loi sur les SA dont le titre III sur les sociétés à capital variable qui donnera un cadre aux coopératives.

1871 Commune de Paris. Réouverture et exploitation par des coopératives ouvrières des ateliers abandonnés par leurs patrons. Mais avec l'écrasement de la Commune et la répression du gouvernement Thiers, les ouvriers sont fusillés ou déportés massivement.

1875 Troisième République. Renaissance du Mouvement ouvrier avec une orientation politique et syndicale.

1879 Le Congrès Ouvrier est défavorable aux coopératives.

1881 Ouverture aux coopératives des marchés de la ville de Paris.

1884 Abandon de l'appartenance aux " associations ouvrières " à cause d'une loi interdisant aux associations d'avoir une activité commerciale. Les coopératives qui se constituent sont presque toutes animées par des militants syndicalistes. Une vingtaine de sociétés coopératives cherchent à se regrouper et à se faire reconnaître publiquement. Naissance de la première Chambre consultative des associations ouvrières de production (ancêtre de la CG Scop). Cette dernière publie le journal Association ouvrière.

1885 Mise en place de l'Ecole de Nîmes (sous la houlette de Charles Gide) qui a constitué pendant des dizaines d'années le haut lieu de la pensée coopérative en France. **1888** Ouverture aux coopératives des marchés de l'Etat et des collectivités publiques.

1892-1895 Création par les Mouvements coopératifs de différents pays de l'Alliance Coopérative. Internationale (ACI). Distinction des différentes branches de la coopération dont celle des producteurs et celle des consommateurs.

1893 Fondation de la Banque coopérative des sociétés ouvrières de production (qui remplace la Société du Crédit au Travail disparue en 1868).

1900 247 coopératives de production.

1910 La coopération de production prend son envol grâce à des regroupements d'ouvriers professionnels dans le bâtiment, le livre ou la transformation des métaux. 500 coopératives, 20 000 sociétaires, 8 000 auxiliaires.

1915 Publication du texte concernant les Scop dans le livre III du Code du Travail.

1919-1920 Eclosion de nombreuses coopératives, en particulier dans le bâtiment, grâce au soutien des marchés publics.

1930-1936 Poussée de création de Scop due à la crise économique et au Front populaire.

1937 Transformation de la Chambre consultative en Confédération générale des Scop.

1938 Création de la Caisse Centrale du crédit coopératif afin de financer le développement des coopératives de production et de consommation.

A la Libération Après la guerre 39-45, renaissance du Mouvement coopératif de production, surtout dans le bâtiment (reconstruction). Parallèlement, naissance du Mouvement des Communautés de travail (Boimondau, Rochebrune…).

1945 Création de la Fédération nationale des Scop du bâtiment et des travaux publics.

1946 Création de l'Union Sociale des Sociétés Coopératives de Consommation et de Production. But : créer, administrer et subventionner des œuvres sociales en faveur des ouvriers et employés des sociétés adhérentes.

1947 Loi Ramadier qui régit toutes les formes de coopération.

Années 60 L'Entente Communautaire, fédération des communautés de travail (52 en 1954, 27 en 1957), se rallie à la CG Scop.

Après 1968 Montée des Scop grâce à « l'esprit de mai ».

1970 Fusion de la Banque coopérative des associations ouvrières de production avec le groupe Crédit coopératif.

1978 Loi permettant la création de Scop-SARL.

De 1978 à 1982 Essor du nombre de Scop et du nombre d'emplois.

1983 1300 coopératives adhèrent à la CG Scop, avec 41 000 salariés dont 24 000 (soit 60 %) sociétaires + environ 200 Scop non adhérentes (ou en cours).

1992 Loi modernisant le statut des coopératives.

1995 Création de la première coopérative d'activités Cap Services.

2001 Loi permettant la création de Scic (Société coopérative d'intérêt collectif).

2002 Caderonne, première Scic agréée.

En 2010, pour mieux refléter la diversité des Scop, présentes dans tous les secteurs d'activité, le Mouvement adopte l'appellation Société coopérative et participative (anciennement Coopérative ouvrière de production).

Annexe 2 : Statut Scop : textes principaux (source les-scop.coop)

- Loi n° 47-1775 du 10 septembre 1947 portant sur le statut de la coopération
- Loi n° 78-763 du 19 juillet 1978 portant sur le statut des sociétés coopératives ouvrières de production (Cf. : Articles L231-1 et suivants du Code de commerce relatifs à la variabilité du capital) modifiée par :
    - Loi n° 84-578 du 9 juillet 1984
    - Loi n° 85-703 du 12 juillet 1985
    - Loi n° 88-15 du 5 janvier 1988
- Loi n° 92-643 du 13 juillet 1992 relative à la modernisation des entreprises coopératives (voir également Instruction du 21 décembre 1992 relative à la modification du régime des sociétés coopératives)

Autres textes spécifiques aux Scop

- **Reconnaissance du statut SCOP** - Décret n° 79-376 du 10 mai 1979 fixant les conditions d'établissement de la liste des Scop (abrogé par le décret n° 93-1231 du 10 novembre 1993) - Décret n° 93-1231 du 10 novembre 1993 relatif à la reconnaissance de la qualité de société coopérative ouvrière de production.
- **Parts sociales** - Décret n° 79-67 du 18 janvier 1979 relatif aux parts sociales émises par les sociétés coopératives ouvrières de production.
- Décret n° 79-558 du 27 juin 1979 relatif à l'application du titre III, chapitre III, de la loi n° 78-763 du 19 juillet 1978 portant sur le statut des sociétés coopératives ouvrières de production et concernant la souscription de parts sociales réservées aux salariés.
- **Epargne salariale** - Décret n° 887-544 du 17 juillet 1987 fixant les conditions d'application de l'ordonnance n° 86-1134 du 21 octobre 1986 relative à l'intéressement et à la participation des salariés aux résultats de l'entreprise et à l'actionnariat des salariés (art. 32 à 35).
- **Révision coopérative** - Arrêté du 29 mars 1989 relatif aux règles particulières de la procédure de révision coopérative dans les sociétés coopératives ouvrières de production.
- **Taxe professionnelle** - Instruction du 25 mars 1993 du SLF relative à la taxe professionnelle.
- **Dirigeants de SCOP** - Directive Unedic n° 31-94 du 23 septembre 1994 relative à la situation des dirigeants de Scop.
- **Marchés publics** - Article 54 du Code des marchés publics attribuant aux Scop un « droit de préférence ».

- **Transformation d'associations en sociétés coopératives** - Article 36 de la loi n° 2001-624 du 17 juillet 2001 relative aux sociétés coopératives d'intérêt collectif (Scic)
- **Société Coopérative Européenne (SCE)**
  Statut de la Société coopérative européenne
    - Décret n°2009-767 du 22 juin 2009 relatif à la société coopérative européenne
    - Loi n° 2008-649 du 3 juillet 2008 portant diverses dispositions d'adaptation du droit des sociétés au droit communautaire
    - Règlement (CE) n° 1435/2003 du Conseil de l'Union européenne du 22 juillet 2003 relatif au statut de la société coopérative européenne (SCE)

  Implication des travailleurs
    - Loi n° 2008-89 du 30 janvier 2008 relative à la mise en œuvre des dispositions communautaires concernant le statut de la société coopérative européenne et la protection des travailleurs salariés en cas d'insolvabilité de l'employeur
    - Directive 2003/72/CE du Conseil de l'Union européenne du 22 juillet 2003 complétant le statut de la société coopérative européenne pour ce qui concerne l'implication des travailleurs

Pour en savoir plus, téléchargez le Guide juridique de la SCE (publié par Coop FR)

Les coopératives emploient plus de 100 millions de femmes et d'hommes, et comptent plus de 800 millions de membres dans le monde.

En juin 2002, l'Organisation internationale du travail (OIT) adopte une recommandation concernant la promotion des coopératives. Il s'agit du premier texte normatif mondial sur les coopératives.

Article 6 : "... les gouvernements devraient mettre en place une politique et un cadre juridique favorables, conformes à la nature et à la fonction des coopératives et fondés sur les valeurs et les principes coopératifs."

L'Alliance Coopérative Internationale (ACI) est une association indépendante et non-gouvernementale qui regroupe, représente et assiste les coopératives du monde entier. Elle a été fondée à Londres en 1895. Ses membres sont des coopératives nationales et internationales de toutes les branches : agriculture, banque, épargne et crédit, énergie, industrie, assurances, pêche, travail, logement, tourisme et consommation. L'ACI compte plus de 248 organisations membres provenant de 92 pays, et représentant quelque 800 millions de personnes du monde entier. Les coopératives de travail associées sont présentes dans le monde entier et dans tous les secteurs d'activité : construction, production industrielle, services généraux, transport, services intellectuels, activités artisanales, santé, services sociaux, etc. Avec la récente transformation de l'économie mondiale, le nombre des coopératives industrielles, artisanales et de services n'a cessé d'augmenter, tant dans les pays en voie de développement que dans les pays industrialisés. Elles sont représentées au plan mondial par le Cicopa, Organisation internationale des coopératives de production industrielles, d'artisanat et de services. Il rassemble aujourd'hui 57 organisations de 39 pays.

CONTRIBUTORS

HABIBULLAH Khan, ***Associate Professor,*** *Graduate School of Business U21 Global, Singapore*

Habibullah Khan teaches Economics and Finance at U21Global, where his teaching and research focus is on Managerial Economics and Global and Regional Economic Development. As Associate Dean of Academic Programs, he is also responsible for all assessment-related matters, including the moderation and publication of students' grades. Khan oversees the development of new subjects and works closely with authors, academic reviewers and U21pedagogica (the review and accreditation agency for U21Global). Prior to joining U21Global, Khan was Associate Professor of Economics at the National University of Singapore from 1997 to 2004. His research areas include development economics, the economies of ASEAN and NIEs, and tourism. He has widely consulted with international organizations, including the World Bank and the ASEAN Secretariat. Khan holds a PhD (Economics) from University of New South Wales, Australia (1980), MA (Economics) from Dhaka University, Bangladesh (1970) and BA (Economics Honours) from Dhaka University, Bangladesh (1969).

✉ *hkhan@u21global.edu.sg*

GURRIB Ikhlaas, ***Professor, Canadian University of Dubai***

Dr. Ikhlaas Gurrib completed his PhD (Finance), and two Master degrees from Australia. He is currently the MBA (Finance) Program Coordinator at the Canadian University of Dubai, which is ranked 3rd among GCC leading universities for its MBA Program. He previously held academic positions in Australia and Saudi Arabia. On top of his industry experience in an Australian leading bank as a finance manager, he is a Senior Associate of the Financial Institute Services of Australasia (FINSIA).

✉ *ikhlaas@cud.ac.ae*

BESSON Dominique, ***Professor, IAE, University of Lille1, France, and Associate Professor, Holy Spirit University of Kaslik (USEK), Lebanon***

Holder of a Ph.D in Business Sciences, Dominique Besson is Full Professor at the Lille 1 University and Head of International Relations at IAE Lille 1 where he delivers Human Resources and Management

courses. His research works revolve around Human Resources and Management notably in regards to SME's. His papers were published in international scientific ranked journals where he is as well member of the editorial review board.
✉ *dbesson@iaelille.fr*

KHALIFE Danielle, ***Assistant Professor, Holy Spirit University of Kaslik (USEK), Lebanon***
Holder of a Ph.D in Business Sciences from the University of Bordeaux IV, she is assistant professor at the Faculty of Business and Commercial Sciences at USEK, where she is a lecturer of Financial Politics, International Finance, and Risk Capital courses. She conducts research in those fields related to market finance and governance at the level of investment capital in Lebanese enterprises.
✉ *daniellekhalife@usek.edu.lb*

SALLOUM Charbel, ***Associate Professor, Holy Spirit University of Kaslik (USEK), Lebanon***
Charbel Salloum is an Associate Professor HDR at the USEK School of Business of the Holy Spirit University of Kaslik where he gives financial markets, portfolio management, technical analysis, and research methodology courses. He has pursued a professional training in the United States, at the New York Stock Exchange (NYSE) and Chicago Mercantile Exchange (CME). His research works revolve around financial markets and governance, notably in regards to financial distress in family business. His papers were published in international scientific ranked journals where he is as well member of the editorial review board. He also is an academic evaluator for Pearson publishing. He is a research fellow at CEREFIGE Lorraine University in France and a visiting Professor at Sorbonne University/Panthéon-Assas, IAE Lyon 3, IAE de Lille 1, IAE de Metz, Lorraine University and The George Washington University.
✉ *charbelsalloum@usek.edu.lb*

AJAKA Jassem, ***Professor***
Julien Jassem AJAKA holds a Ph.D since 1997 in Nuclear Physics. He has worked for more than 8 years in financial markets as senior consultant at a council cabinet in Paris. He is also holder of 2 Masters: one in Financial Markets and Asset Management, and another one in management. He came back to Lebanon in 2004, taught at different private universities and advised several Lebanese banks and financial institutions as well as politicians before he got in 2008 a full professor position in Physics at the

Lebanese University – Faculty of Sciences. Currently he is registered in France for a PhD in Economics; which main topic is: "Strong Euro and its Impact on European Economies: A Marco-econometric approach". Jassem has more than 30 publications in Physics, and Human Sciences and speaks fluently 4 languages: Arabic, English, French and Esperanto.
✉ *julienajaka@gmail.com*

AZOURY Nehmé, ***Associate Professor, Holy Spirit University of Kaslik (USEK), Lebanon***
Holder of a PhD and a Master in Business (Paris XI University and Holy Spirit University of Kaslik (USEK)), Nehme Azoury is Associate Professor and Dean of the Faculty of Business and Commercial Sciences at the Holy Spirit University of Kaslik (Lebanon), where he teaches Strategic Management and Corporate Governance. He is the Secretary General of the Arab Society of Faculties of Business Administration and one of the eight members of the EDUNIVERSAL Scientific Committee, which represents Eurasia and the Middle East. He has linked the worlds of business and academia, by working as Consultant with many reputable companies before dedicating himself to teaching. He was a visiting Professor at various foreign universities; such as, Paris II, Euromed-Marseille, La Rochelle, Lyon 3 and The George Washington University, which honored him with an appreciation award. He has written numerous academic papers and is Editor-in-Chief of The Arab Economic and Business Journal, and the e-journal *La Revue Libanaise de Gestion et d'Économie* (The Lebanese Journal of Business and Economics).
✉ *nehmeazoury@usek.edu.lb*

DUYCK Jean-Yves, ***University Professor, La Rochelle University, France***
Since 2005, Jean-Yves Duyck has been running the Group of Age and Time Management at AGRH and International Institute of Social Audit Office. On a national level, he had constant and important administrative responsibilities at the CNU for fourteen years, eleven of which were spent as the Section 6 and CNRS Section 37 Vice-President. He is a member of CTPMESR and an AERES expert. On a local level, he founded the Commerce and Distribution IUP of La Rochelle and is a Management Evaluator at The UFR Law Office and The ULR Management Office. Jean-Yves Duyck is an elected member of the University Scientific Council and The UFR Council. He sat and reported upon many Theses Juries and published the special Seniors Management Edition of *The Management et Avenir journal (n°6, January 2006).* He co-wrote, with

Stéphane Bellini, the book *En âge de travailler – Recherches sur les âges au travail* (Vuibert 2009). He participated in many seminars and his academic papers have been published in reputable journals on management; two of his research works were published (Vuibert) in March 2009 and August 2010.

✉ *jyduyck@univ-lr.fr*

SASSINE Mario, ***Assistant Professor, Holy Spirit University of Kaslik (USEK), Lebanon***

Holder of a PhD and Master in Business Administration from University of Montesquieu –Bordeaux IV, Mario is Assistant Professor at the Faculty of Business and Commercial Sciences of the Holy Spirit University of Kaslik (Lebanon), where he teaches Financial Accounting and the Principles of Management. Responsible for research and development of the International Research Center in Managerial and Economic Applications (CIRAME), his actual concerns in research are focused on themes of firms and family dynasties, social auditing and corporate governance. The theoretical anchoring of his research concerns those of organizational finance and behavioral finance.

✉ *mariosassine@usek.edu.lb*

AJINA Aymen, ***Assistant Professor, HEC-Business School, University of Liège (Belgium); ISG of Sousse (Tunisia)***

Holder of a Ph.D in Management from HEC School of Management at the University of Liege and the ISG University of Sousse, he is an assistant professor at the University of Sousse, Tunisia. His research focuses on financial reporting, corporate governance, and market liquidity. He published in scientific journals and has participated to several international conferences.

✉ *aymen.ajina@doct.ulg.ac.be*

MERCIER-SUISSA Catherine, ***Associate Professor, Université Jean Moulin Lyon III – IAE - Laboratoire Magellan***

Assistant Director of the IAE, Catherine Mercier-Suissa is Associate Professor in Economic Sciences. She is also director of the Centre French-Italian International Management at IAE Lyon 3 University and responsible for the program COMEX (Trade) of the International Management master at the IAE.

✉ *catherine.mercier-suissa@univ-lyon3.fr*

ALEXANDRE-LECLAIR Laurice, ***Associate Professor,*** *Sorbonne Paris Cité/Paris Descartes University, France*
Associate Professor at Sorbonne Paris Cité/Paris Descartes University, Laurice Alexandre Leclair's main interests are in the international development of SMEs, social entrepreneurship and female entrepreneurship. She has initiated the creation of the association SIFE Paris Descartes (Students in Free Enterprise), and she is the Pedagogical Advisor for Social Entrepreneurship Projects. Laurice has occupied the position of Coordinator of the Business Faculty and Information System at the French University in Egypt for 2 years (2009-2011), an assignment for the French Foreign Affairs Ministry. She is the author of a book about distribution partnership between groups and SMEs in 2007, Vuibert Edition.
✉ *laurice.alexandre-leclair@parisdescartes.fr*

Index of Texts in English

INDEX DES TEXTES EN FRANÇAIS